KT-521-850

THE ROLE OF HUMAN RIGHTS
IN FOREIGN POLICY

WORCESTER COLLEGE
OF TECHNOLOGY

0095 180

Also by Peter R. Baehr

POLICY ANALYSIS AND POLICY INNOVATION (*editor with Björn Wittrock*)

THE NETHERLANDS AND THE UNITED NATIONS: Selected Issues (*editor with Monique Castermans-Holleman*)

THE UNITED NATIONS: Reality and Ideal (*with Leon Gordenker*)

THE UNITED NATIONS IN THE 1990s (*with Leon Gordenker*)

The Role of Human Rights in Foreign Policy

Peter R. Baehr

Professor of Human Rights, Utrecht University
and
Director of the Netherlands Institute of Human Rights

Foreword by Peter Kooijmans

Second Edition

© Peter R. Baehr 1994, 1996
Foreword © Peter Kooijmans 1994

All rights reserved. No reproduction, copy or transmission of
this publication may be made without written permission.

No paragraph of this publication may be reproduced, copied or
transmitted save with written permission or in accordance with
the provisions of the Copyright, Designs and Patents Act 1988,
or under the terms of any licence permitting limited copying
issued by the Copyright Licensing Agency, 90 Tottenham Court
Road, London W1P 9HE.

Any person who does any unauthorised act in relation to this
publication may be liable to criminal prosecution and civil
claims for damages.

First edition 1994
Second edition 1996

Published by
MACMILLAN PRESS LTD
Houndmills, Basingstoke, Hampshire RG21 6XS
and London
Companies and representatives
throughout the world

ISBN 0–333–68342–0 hardcover
ISBN 0–333–66992–4 paperback

A catalogue record for this book is available
from the British Library.

10   9   8   7   6   5   4   3   2   1
05   04   03   02   01   00   99   98   97   96

Printed in Great Britain by
Antony Rowe Ltd
Chippenham, Wiltshire

Contents

Foreword

Much has changed in the field of human rights and foreign policy during the last few years. The confrontation between East and West, of which the human rights issue was a preponderant part, has – at least for the time being – disappeared. As a consequence in this relationship, the human rights debate has lost its political overtones. That does not mean, however, that human rights have become less politicized. During the preparation of the World Conference on Human Rights, held in June 1993 in Vienna, the issue of universality or cultural relativism loomed large. And in spite of the fact that in the concluding document of the Conference this controversy apparently was solved by the adoption of a consensus text, the fact that there was no real meeting of minds is evidenced by the controversies about the establishment of the post of High Commissioner of Human Rights during the 1993 session of the UN General Assembly, although the World Conference had recommended this without open opposition.

Moreover, in a number of countries, violations of human rights are either openly perpetrated by the authorities or are wilfully condoned. An active policy – either bilaterally or multilaterally with regard to such violations – is as necessary as it used to be in the past. The establishment of monitoring mechanisms can play a useful role in this respect.

What has become more important than in the past is the promotion of human rights by rendering advisory services. This is not only true for the countries in Central and Eastern Europe, where new Governments have committed themselves to the rule of law, but also in other parts of the world where authoritarian or dictatorial rulers had to make place for democratically elected Governments. This opens new vistas for an active policy focused on a better respect for human rights. For we should realize that respect for human rights is not only a question of political will but that good governance, which is so closely linked with the human rights issue, asks for a structural approach.

Professor Baehr has meticulously scrutinized the various factors which determine foreign policy in the field of human rights. In doing so he has also taken into account other factors which play a preponderant role in foreign policy. In a world where there are new challenges, but at the same time reasons for serious concern, this book makes thought-provoking reading for all those who have committed themselves to the cause of human rights.

DR PETER KOOIJMANS
Minister for Foreign Affairs
of the Kingdom of the Netherlands
(1993–94)

Preface

This book is about the relationship between human rights and foreign policy. Part I discusses this relationship in general; part II deals with a number of specific countries and regions.

The perspective of this book is a blend of realism and optimism. Realism means recognition of the fact that human rights are by no means the only consideration guiding foreign policy, plus a full awareness of the fact that human rights are still being violated in many parts of the world. More optimistic is the assumption of the universality of international human rights standards, or of at least a growing consensus in that direction. Non-governmental organizations play a significant role in this. Though written from a 'pro human rights' point of view, a genuine effort has been made to avoid subjective bias in the treatment of the subject. The personal views of the author are expressed in the concluding chapter.

The basis for this book was laid during a fellowship at the Netherlands Institute for Advanced Study (NIAS) in Wassenaar in the 1980s, which led to the publication of *Mensenrechten: Bestanddeel van het Buitenlands Beleid*, published in Dutch in 1989 by Boom Meppel. Boom has graciously given permission to use the original Dutch text as a basis for this book. The text has been fully revised and updated. For obvious reasons this is especially true for Chapter 8 which deals with the former Soviet Union.

Saskia Bal of the Netherlands Institute of Human Rights (SIM) helped in collecting the necessary source material, while Annelies Bos, Nelki Lauret and Jacqueline Smith, also of SIM, were most helpful in the preparation of the manuscript. I also want to thank Ineke Boerefijn, Monique Castermans, David Forsythe, Wolfgang Heinz, Johannes van der Klaauw, Yvonne Klerk, Cecilia Medina, Sally Morphet, Tiemo Oostenbrink, Alfred Pijpers, William Wallace and

Leo Zwaak, who read parts of the manuscript. The full responsibility for the use of the commentary and the source material rests of course solely with the author.

PETER R. BAEHR

Heemstede, the Netherlands
August 1993

Preface to the Second Edition

This second edition of *The Role of Human Rights in Foreign Policy* has been marginally revised and brought up to date. The section on European cooperation has been more substantially revised. New developments since August 1993, such as the appointment of the United Nations High Commissioner for Human Rights, the coming into force of the Maastricht Treaty on European Union and the renaming of the Conference into the Organization for Security and Cooperation in Europe, have been covered. A number of new references have been added.

As this revision is being completed, it is obvious that human rights remain very much on the international political agenda. Political developments such as the sad events in the former Yugoslavia and in Rwanda belong very much to the themes covered in this book. It is tragic but true that the international community has not yet been able to find effective ways of preventing or solving gross human rights violations. The activities of non-governmental organizations and of international governmental agencies to combat such violations remain as necessary as ever.

Saskia Bal and Maaike Hogenkamp of the Netherlands Institute of Human Rights (SIM) were a great help in collecting and bringing up-to-date source material. I also want to thank Ineke Boerefijn, Johannes van der Klaauw and Cecilia Medina who checked and commented on part of the revised text. The responsibility for the final result remains with the author.

Heemstede, the Netherlands　　　　　　　　PETER R. BAEHR
January 1996

Part I
General

1 Introduction

'The rights of man, human rights, or fundamental rights, are names given to those elementary rights which are considered to be indispensable for the development of the individual.'[1] Thus begins the memorandum, *Human Rights and Foreign Policy*, which was published in 1979 by the Dutch Ministry of Foreign Affairs. With the cited text the ministry made a commendable effort at clarifying its views on the subject; it opted for emphasizing the rights of *individuals*.

In this introductory chapter I will discuss various aspects of what is commonly referred to as human rights and their relationship to foreign policy. My purpose is not to given an exhaustive survey of all existing definitions. Many of those are, as an American scholar has observed, of a rather abstract nature.[2] The following examples will illustrate this point. The political philosopher Maurice Cranston refered to human rights as 'something that pertains to all men at all times. Therefore, it cannot be justified in the way we justify rights that are earned or are acquired by the enactment of special roles; human rights are not bought, nor are they created by any other specific contractual undertaking ... They belong to a man simply because he is man.'[3] The Australian political scientist Hedley Bull called human rights 'rights attaching to human beings as such, rather than to this or that class of human beings. They are thought to be enjoyed by all human beings, to be enjoyed by human beings only and to be enjoyed by them equally.'[4] For our purposes it is sufficient to note that the subject refers to rights that belong to human beings – rights that have a status of their own. They are considered to be of greater importance than other rights. For that reason they are called human rights or rights of man.

Human rights have a place of their own in foreign policy. More traditional objectives of foreign policy, such as the

3

protection of national security or the promotion of foreign
trade, are based on material interests of the state. Human
rights differ from other objectives of foreign policy in that
they do not refer to such direct material interests.
Governments that want to promote human rights abroad
do not set themselves an easy task. They have to face
difficult choices of policies and priorities. There are, nevertheless, governments who have decided to include the
promotion of human rights among their foreign policy
objectives.

RIGHTS OF THE INDIVIDUAL

By way of commentary to the quoted definition, the Dutch
government has noted that there are certain rights which are
exercised by groups of people. For example, reference was
made to the right of association and the right of assembly,
the right of ethnic and cultural minorities to preserve their
own language and culture and the right of peoples to self-determination. In the view of the Dutch Foreign Ministry, the
reason for recognizing self-determination as a human right is
that its realization is regarded as an essential precondition
for the development of the individual in a manner worthy of
human dignity.[5]

This emphasis on the individual represents a rather
typical *western* approach to the concept of human rights. I
shall return to this when discussing the subject of cultural
relativism (Chapter 2). At this stage it should be emphasized that there is another view that holds that collective
rights derive their value from the collectivity as such and
therefore need not necessarily serve the development of the
individual. Thus it is no accident that the most important
African human rights document is called 'African Charter
of Human *and Peoples*' Rights' (emphasis added). I will
return later to the consequences of this view. Here it is
simply noted that the development of the individual provides an important background to the notion of human
rights, but not necessarily the only one.

BASIC DOCUMENTS

The two most important basic documents for human rights are of western origin: the Virginia Bill of Rights of 1776 which was incorporated in 1791 in the United States Constitution, and the French Declaration of the Rights of Man and Citizen of 1789. Both documents contain a list of human rights in the sense of individual liberties. Many of these rights are based on the writings of political philosophers such as John Locke, Montesquieu and Jean-Jacques Rousseau.[6]

The preamble to the Charter of the United Nations mentions explicitly the notion of fundamental human rights. Article 1, paragraph 3 calls as one of the purposes of the United Nations: 'to achieve international co-operation in solving international problems of an economic, social, cultural, or humanitarian character, and in promoting and encouraging respect for human rights and for fundamental freedoms for all without distinction as to race, sex, language or religion'. This led in 1948 to the adoption by the General Assembly of the Universal Declaration of Human Rights (see appendix, pp. 171–78). This Declaration was proclaimed as a 'common standard of achievement for all peoples and all nations'.

Human rights were incorporated in these UN documents as a reaction to the outrageous crimes against humanity committed by the national socialists in Germany between 1933 and 1945. The torture and killing of more than six million Jews, gypsies, homosexuals and political opponents was the largest-scale violation of fundamental human rights in modern times. Concepts such as 'genocide' and 'crimes against humanity' are inseparably linked to this period in world history.

The Universal Declaration contains a list of the most important human rights. These include the following civil and political rights:

- the right to life, liberty and security of person (article 3);

- the prohibition of slavery (article 4);
- the prohibition of torture (article 5);
- the prohibition of arbitrary arrest, detention or exile (article 9);
- the right to a fair trial (article 10);
- the right to freedom of movement (article 13);
- the right to property (article 17);
- the right to freedom of thought, conscience and religion (article 18);
- the right to freedom of opinion and expression (article 19);
- the right to freedom of assembly and association (article 20);
- the right to participate in the government of one's country (article 21).

The Universal Declaration also mentions some important social and economic rights:

- the right to work (article 23);
- the right to an adequate standard of living, including food, clothing, housing and medical care (article 25);
- the right to education (article 26).

Cultural rights include the right to participate in the cultural life of one's community, to share in scientific advancement and the right to the protection of the moral and material interests resulting from one's scientific, literary or artistic production (article 27).

These rights have been elaborated in two legally binding international treaties which were adopted by the General Assembly in 1966: the International Covenant on Civil and Political Rights and the International Covenant on Economic, Social and Cultural Rights. They differ from the Universal Declaration in that they do not include the right to seek asylum, the right to nationality and the right to property. The Covenant on Civil and Political Rights adds to the Universal Declaration that all persons deprived of their liberty shall be treated with humanity and with respect for the inherent dignity of the human person and that no one shall be liable to be tried or punished again for an offence for which he has already been finally convicted or acquitted. Both covenants mention explicitly in article 1 the right of all peoples to self-determination. The covenants are more detailed than the Universal Declaration and contain a number of specific restrictions. Both entered into force in 1976. The Covenant on Civil and Political Rights has now (winter 1996) been ratified by 130 states, the Covenant on Economic, Social and Cultural Rights by 131 states.

GOVERNMENT ABSTENTION

The fundamental rights and freedoms emphasize the need for *government abstention* with regard to the rights of the individual. A government is not allowed to torture and should not allow its servants to do so. It may not interfere in the right of people to associate and to assemble freely; it may not interfere in the freedom of the press and freedom of expression.

But that is not the whole story. Sometimes a government must do something in order to guarantee that the rights and freedoms can actually be exercised. For example, the right to a fair trial can only be realized if there are sufficient trained lawyers to conduct such trials and if the judicial authorities have the necessary technical means at their disposal. Sometimes freedom of assembly can only be exercised under police protection against political opponents. The right to participate in the government of one's country, 'directly or through freely chosen representatives' (Universal Declaration of Human Rights, article 21), requires the organization of free and secret elections by the government. Training facilities, libraries and other provisions will normally be supplied by the government.[7] Full government abstention is, in other words, not enough to guarantee respect for these rights and liberties. The opposite may be true.

In the case of social and economic rights, the need for government intervention is even greater. The realization of such rights as the right to work, the right to education, the right to medical care and the right to social security is nowadays unthinkable without some measure of government involvement. There may be political differences of view about the extent of this government involvement, but the nineteenth century idea of the 'night watchman state' has been abandoned.

THREE 'GENERATIONS' OF HUMAN RIGHTS

Human rights literature usually distinguishes among three 'generations' of human rights. The first generation refers to civil and political rights – the 'classic' human rights. Economic, social and cultural rights belong to the second generation. The third generation contains a number of collective rights which have received increasing attention in recent years.[8] Such rights are the following:

- the right to development;
- the right to peace;
- the right to a clean natural environment;
- the right to one's own natural resources;
- the right to one's own cultural heritage.

The latter two rights are usually considered to be part of the common heritage of mankind. Some of these third-generation rights, which have been mainly emphasized by the former communist and the Third World states, are rather controversial in the eyes of the West. They have been criticized for their vagueness and lack of clarity. Take, for example, the right to peace; most people will be in favour of an abstract notion of peace, but that notion acquires real meaning only when such questions are answered as: peace under what circumstances? and at what price? It is, moreover, unclear who could exercise such a right to peace – individuals, groups or states – and how it can be enforced. On the other hand, Katarina Tomasevski has a point when she argues that the conception of peace as a human right might help in 'raising public awareness that everyone has a stake in peace-keeping, widening public support for disarmament policy'.[9]

The term 'generations' is somewhat unfortunate. It suggests a succession of phenomena, whereby a new generation takes the place of the previous one. That is, however, not the case with the three 'generations' of human rights. On the contrary. The idea is rather that the three 'generations' exist and should be respected simultaneously.

Finally, there is the curious phenomenon that one particular right – that of self-determination – belongs both to the first and the second 'generation'. It is mentioned in the International Covenant on Civil and Political Rights and in the International Covenant on Economic, Social and Cultural Rights. The reason is that the African and Asian states, which already were in the majority when the two treaties were adopted by the General Assembly in 1966, wanted in this way to emphasize the importance of this right.

HIERARCHY OF HUMAN RIGHTS

It is not common practice to put human rights in any hierarchical order. At the United Nations it is even frowned upon to call certain human rights more important than others. Nevertheless, there exists clearly some kind of difference between them. Thus there are rights which, according to article 4 of the International Covenant on Civil and Political Rights, may not be derogated from, even in a state of public emergency. Such rights include the protection of the right to life, the prohibition of torture, the prohibition of slavery and the freedom of thought, conscience and religion, but none of the social and economic rights. Other human rights treaties name different rights as 'non-derogable'.

In this context it should be mentioned that international experts meeting in Syracusa, Italy in 1984, tried to further define the conditions and grounds for permissible limita-

tions and derogations of human rights. The point of departure was that such conditions and grounds should themselves be clearly defined and strongly limited.[10] So far, these
proposals have not been put in an international legally
binding treaty.

Another useful distinction is that between principal rights
and other rights. Principal rights are rights that are necessary for a dignified human existence and which therefore
should receive absolute protection. Among such principal
rights are the right to life and personal integrity, which includes freedom from slavery, servitude and torture, arbitrary arrest, discrimination and other acts that violate
human dignity. Freedom of religion and freedom of expression are also considered as principal rights. Some writers
include among the principal rights the right to adequate
food, clothing, housing and medical care.

The distinction between principal rights and other rights
may be of importance to policy making. A government may
react more sharply, if it is confronted by a violation of principal rights elsewhere. This calls for a clear and sharply
delineated definition of such rights. If too many rights are
considered to be principal rights, the concept loses its
significance. This is called inflation of terms.[11]

VERTICAL AND HORIZONTAL EFFECT

So far, we have dealt with human rights in a 'vertical'
meaning, i.e. to protect individuals or groups against unjust
government interference. There is, however, also a 'horizontal' meaning which refers to relations *among* citizens. In
such cases, it is the task of the government to protect the individual against violations of his rights by others. In the
memorandum of the Dutch Ministry of Foreign Affairs,
cited before, the example is given of the right to life and
the right to liberty of the individual, which implies that the
government must endeavour to protect people against
homicide and deprivation of life by their fellow human
beings. 'In more abstract terms it can be said that the liberty

of every individuals has its bounds at the line where the exercise of such liberty would constitute a violation of the liberty of others.'[12]

In foreign policy this horizontal effect is less important than the vertical one, except where a government has knowingly failed to give certain individuals such protection or when it helps directly or indirectly such violations of human rights in its own country or abroad. This happens, for instance, in the case of so-called 'death squads' which eliminate political opponents under direct instructions of a government ('vertical effect') or with its tacit consent ('horizontal effect').

2 Universality and Cultural Relativism

Universal human rights instruments are based on the assumption that they reflect universally accepted norms of behaviour. This is important, among other things, for the supervisory role of the United Nations in ensuring that these international standards are respected. Unless human rights – or at least a nucleus of such rights – are universally valid, the United Nations can have no basis on which to found its supervision activities.

That assumption governed the approval in 1948 of the Universal Declaration of Human Rights by the General Assembly of the United Nations. It states in the beginning of its preamble that the 'recognition of the inherent dignity and of the equal and inalienable rights of all members of the human family is the foundation of freedom, justice and peace in the world'. That is also the foundation of the two international covenants on human rights, which were adopted in 1966.

However, the acceptance of those texts does not mean that the universal nature of human rights has been generally accepted. Among often-heard criticisms of the Universal Declaration are the following:[1]

— it was drafted at a time when most Third World nations were still under colonial domination; developing nations that later incorporated the standards of the Universal Declaration in their national constitutions or accepted them as members of the Organization of American States or the Organization of African Unity, did so under western pressure;[2]
— furthermore, the rights contained in the Universal Declaration are said to reflect mainly western ideo-

logical views, rather than values dominant in non-
western societies;[3]
— the Declaration uses an individualistic approach to
human rights, which is supposedly not suitable for
societies that emphasize collective values.

CULTURAL RELATIVISM

Adherents of the notion of 'cultural relativism' go even
further.[4] They argue that local or regional cultural traditions in the fields of religion, politics, economics and law
determine the existence and scope of civil and political
rights enjoyed by individuals in a given society.[5] It is further
argued that ethical and moral standards differ in different
places and times. These differences can only be understood
against the background of the different cultural contexts
these norms and values are part of. This cultural context is
also assumed to determine the amount of attention that is
given to human rights. There is not supposed to exist something like a universal morality, because the world has always
been characterized by a plurality of cultures.[6]

This view can have far-reaching consequences for the validity of international human rights standards. If all
depends on the local cultural context, there is little room
left for the universal validity of international human rights
standards. It is not surprising that cultural relativism, especially its extreme consequences, has been bitterly opposed.
Rhoda Howard, a Canadian political scientist, has called it
'an ideological tool to serve the interests of powerful
emergent groups'.[7]

Even those who do not adhere to the notion of cultural
relativism must admit that the implementation of human
rights in different cultural situations implies that in some
cases certain human rights will be more strongly emphasized than others. That is not necessarily wrong. It has, for
example, often been pointed out that it makes little sense to
emphasize freedom of the press in a society where most
people don't know how to read or write. Therefore one may

well accept Donnelly's notion of 'weak cultural relativism'. He considers culture to be an important source of the validity of a moral right or moral rule; it serves in his view as a check on potential excesses of universalism.[8] This does not mean, however, that 'core rights', i.e. rights dealing with the integrity of the human person, may be harmed. Among those rights are the right to life, the right not to be tortured or to undergo cruel, inhuman or degrading treatment or punishment and the right to freedom of opinion. Most adherents of the notion of cultural relativism agree that these rights should be respected everywhere.

WESTERN ORIGIN

How should one view the notion of universality, as contained in the Universal Declaration of Human Rights? There is little doubt that the idea of the protection of fundamental human rights was first mentioned in western writings. It has its roots in western philosophy and western ways of thinking, with the inclusion of Marxism. The question is whether in the course of time these rights have developed into universal norms of behaviour, which are accepted by human beings with different cultural backgrounds all over the world.

The desire to protect the rights of the individual belongs to the best western traditions, in which human rights relate primarily to rights of individuals which should not be violated by any other individual, group or authority. Here lies a crucial difference with dominant non-western approaches. Donnelly sees the emphasis on the individual as one of the most important differences between modern western and non-western views of human dignity.[9] He argues that the protection of the individual against the demands of society was originally not part of traditional non-western thinking. This does not necessarily mean, however, that in modern times no truly 'universal' norms could have been developed. It is at least conceivable that conceptions of human rights, which were originally western, have been accepted or will be accepted by non-western societies. What counts is the fact that though the protection of individual rights is based on western ideas, this does not exclude such ideas being adopted by others and developed into norms that are universally valid.

There are indications that the latter is indeed what has happened – at least on the level of governments and other political elites. Almost all governments, whatever their ideological or cultural background, condemn systematic and gross violations of human rights, such as genocide, torture or involuntary disappearances. Governments only rarely deny that international human rights standards apply to their country. This is also true for fundamentalist regimes such as that of the Islamic Republic Iran. The Iranian delegate at the United Nations has stated that, in the event of conflict between obligations stemming from international human rights treaties and the directives of the Koran, the latter should prevail.[10] But in practice Iran has shown itself willing to defend its policies before the UN Commission on Human Rights on the basis of those very same human rights treaties. The appeal by the late religious leader of Iran, the Ayatolla Khomeiny, to kill Salman Rushdie, the writer who was accused of blasphemy of the prophet Mohammed in his book *Satanic Verses*, shows, however, that the last word on the question of the universality of norms has not yet been spoken.

No member-state of the United Nations voted in 1948 against adoption of the Universal Declaration of Human Rights. Eight states – the Soviet Union and five of its allies, plus Saudi Arabia and South Africa – abstained. One of the reasons why the Soviet Union abstained was that it felt that the Universal Declaration paid too little attention to the importance of the maintenance of national sovereignty. Soviet delegate Andrej Vishinkij rejected the notion that there existed rights of the individual beyond the context of the state.[11] The Soviet Union also held views of its own with regard to the issue of freedom of opinion, which should, for instance, not include the expression of fascist or racist views.[12] Saudi Arabia's abstention was based on its rejection of including under freedom of religion the right of *changing* one's religion. The latter is not permitted to a religious Moslim.

Since 1948, the principles of the Universal Declaration have been repeatedly reaffirmed in international gatherings, such as the world conferences on human rights held in Teheran in 1968 and in Vienna in June 1993. Governments have not distanced themselves from the Declaration. On the contrary, they pay at least lipservice to its principles. Lipservice – 'the respect that vice pays to virtue' – shows that no government is willing to admit that it violates international human rights norms. The normative standard is accepted in theory, though often not in practice.

ELABORATION IN OTHER HUMAN RIGHTS INSTRUMENTS

The importance of the Declaration has been repeatedly reaffirmed by UN organs. In the Declaration on the Granting of Independence to Colonial Countries and Peoples (1960), in the Declaration on the Elimination of All Forms of Racial Discrimination (1965) and in countless other declarations and resolutions an appeal is made to the states to adhere to the rules of the Universal Declaration of Human Rights. In 1968 the Proclamation of Teheran was adopted which says that the Universal Declaration affirms a common understanding of the peoples of the world concerning the inalienable and inviolable rights of all members of the human family and constitutes an *obligation* for the members of the international community. The second World Conference on Human Rights, held in Vienna in 1993, emphasized that the Universal Declaration is 'the source of inspiration and has been the basis for the United Nations in making advances in standard setting as contained in the existing international human rights instruments'.[13] Increasingly the Universal Declaration, or at least some of its provisions, has become part of international customary law.[14]

Parts of the Declaration have been elaborated in a large number of international treaties which came into being under the auspices of the United Nations and which have been adhered to by many states in the world: on the status of refugees and stateless persons, the political rights of women, the nationality of married women, the prohibition of slavery, slave trade and forced labour, the prohibition of discrimination against women, the prohibition of racial discrimination, the rights of the child, etc. The Convention against Torture and Other Cruel, Inhuman or Degrading Treatment or Punishment, which was adopted in 1984 and came into force in 1987, is an example of an international legal instrument originating from principles that were first formulated in the Universal Declaration.[15]

The often-heard view that certain human rights are not (or not yet) applicable to non-western societies is a reflection of a rather paternalistic way of thinking: 'Freedom of expression is important to us, westerners, but you people in the developing world have not yet reached that stage.' Thus it is often said that developing nations should first provide for basic commodities, such as food and medicine. As long as these basic means are not sufficiently available, it is hardly necessary to guarantee respect for civil and political rights. Especially repressive regimes often argue that there is no need for the protection of fundamental civil and political rights in their countries while the population is undernourished and the country economically underdeveloped. They pretend to emphasize instead the development of socioeconomic rights.

There is, however, some justified grounds for suspicion if such arguments are put forward by *governments*. It has never been demonstrated that a restriction of civil and political rights contributes to the economic development of a country. The only objective it does contribute to is the maintenance of the repressive regime itself! Also the victims of repression rarely argue for the right of their government to repress them. On the contrary, the acceptance of universal human rights seems to be much more universal than oppressive governments often claim. Moreover, the two UN covenants on human rights impose different obligations on the states parties. The respect for civil and political rights is not made dependent on the degree of economic development of a state. In most cases, there does not exist a logical connection between the recognition of certain civil and political rights on the one hand, and the degree of economic development on the other. There is no reason why, for example, the right not to be tortured should not equally apply to rich and to poor countries.

If one wanted to make such a logical connection, the reasoning should, rather, be reversed and provide a *positive* relationship between the two sets of rights. For example, the achievement of fair wages and the right to safe and healthy working conditions may well depend on the right to freedom of assembly and association, i.e. the right to form trade unions. The right to have free and secret elections may contribute to an improvement of living conditions in countries that are governed by corrupt or inefficient dictators. Human rights are intended to protect the weak members of societies, the dissidents, those who want to oppose their own governments. There is no logical reason why that idea should be less valid for non-western societies.

A good example of the current debate on the universality of human rights is provided by the case of Indonesia. The Indonesian government often claims that with regard to human rights Indonesia has it own set of values which are supposedly different from universal human rights standards. However, Adnan Buyung Nasution has shown in his doctoral dissertation that basic notions of human rights were universally accepted by the democratically elected *Konstituante*, which in the late 1950s was preparing a new constitution for Indonesia, until it was disbanded by President Sukarno. He acknowledges that the present prevailing notion on human rights in Indonesia is that they represent western values and that Indonesia has its own norms of human rights, derived from the state philosophy of *Pancasila* (the reigning state ideology). The debates in the *Konstituante* show, however, quite the opposite:

[T]he Konstituante unanimously appreciated the universal validity of human rights as inherent in human nature
and existing in every human civilization. It was generally
believed that if human rights were negated then man
would lose his humanity. Human rights were considered
to be the objective of the state: the state was considered
to exist for man and not man for the state.[16]

The forceful interference by President Sukarno ended
the *Konstituante* and its freely expressed adherence to the
notion of universal human rights. Under President Suharto,
who took over from Sukarno in 1968, human rights have
continued to be violated, though his government also tends
to pay lipservice to the notion of the universality of human
rights.[17]

What happened in Indonesia can be considered illustra-
tive of the situation in many parts of the world. The acceptance of the universality of human rights standards is a
notion that may be uncomfortable to oppressive governments. It is, however, generally adhered to by their victims.

REGIONAL ARRANGEMENTS

Besides global arrangements, there exists a number of regional treaties relating to human rights. The most important are the *European Convention for the Protection of Human
Rights and Fundamental Freedoms* (1950), the *American
Convention on Human Rights* (1969) and the *African Charter
on Human Rights and Peoples' Rights* (1981). In 1961, the
European Social Charter was adopted, which contains important social and economic rights relating to the right to work,
trade unions, protection of employees, vocational training
and migrant workers. Most of the members of the Council
of Europe are party to this Charter.

What is the nature of the relationship between global and
regional human rights treaties? Often, they deal with the
same subjects, though worded differently and with a different scope. Regional arrangements are meant to particular-
ize or sharpen universally valid standards with reference to

a specific geographical region. They are not meant to conflict with, but rather to reinforce, each other. Thus the aim of achieving an international guarantee for the protection of the rights and freedoms of all people should be realized. If there is a conflict, global standards should prevail.

Of all the protection systems the European Convention on Human Rights has the most elaborate supervision mechanism. It provides for a system of individual complaints and the possibility of having these complaints dealt with (by the European Commission for Human Rights and the European Court of Human Rights). In addition, every state party can refer to the Commission for Human Rights any alleged breach of the Convention by another state party. The American Convention on Human Rights contains similar, somewhat less far-reaching provisions. The African Charter on Human and Peoples' Rights is the least far-reaching of the three conventions.

In the past, the East European states did not belong to any regional system for the protection of human rights. However, after the fall of communism many of those states have acceded to, or are in the process of acceding to, the European Convention on Human Rights. For Asia and the Pacific no regional human rights arrangements have been adopted, so far. This is mainly because of the great diversity of cultures within that geographical region. It is no coincidence that there does not exist a regional international organization for Asia, along the lines of the Council of Europe, the Organization of American States and the Organization of African Unity. The nations of Asia and the Pacific seem to have too little in common to agree on the principles of such an organization.

CONCLUSION

There is no doubt that the concept of human rights is interpreted differently according to its political and cultural context. In the past, a distinction was made between 'East' and 'West', meaning the communist as opposed to the western-democratic states. Since the demise of communism, the major division remains between the 'South' and the 'North' – the distinction between the poor, underdeveloped, mainly Asian and African states and the industrialized West European and North American states.

The differences between East and West were in the emphasis they put on the rights of society as a whole versus individual rights, on economic and social rights versus civil and political rights, and on the protection of national sovereignty versus a strengthening of international supervision. The differences between the South and the North relate mainly to the importance that is attached to the right of self-determination, peoples' rights in general and the emphasis that is put, for example in the African Charter for Human Rights and Peoples' Rights, on duties toward society as well as individual rights.

These differences are not static in nature, but evolve over time. Thus, attitudes towards human rights have changed from Stalin's reign over the Soviet Union to that of Gorbachev and that of Yeltsin over present-day Russia. In western countries views about certain economic and social rights are by no means static. Also, the various 'camps' are not closed entities. Within each 'camp' there are differences of opinion and interpretation over the importance to be accorded to certain specific human rights.

In its preamble, the Universal Declaration of Human Rights is proclaimed as a 'common standard of achievement'. It assumes the universality of norms on which that common standard should be based. There does not yet exist full agreement on the nature of those norms, but it would seem correct to speak of an 'emerging consensus'.[18] This 'emerging consensus' provides an opportunity for a debate on the manner in which the norms that are contained in international declarations and conventions can be best implemented. Such a debate and the consensus that, it is hoped, may emerge from that debate are indispensable conditions for arriving at a greater respect for human rights in all parts of the world.

3 Policy Choices

A policy of human rights means a choice among priorities. It means that a government will have to decide whether and when it will give a higher priority to human rights over other foreign policy considerations, such as national security, foreign trade and development cooperation. Such policy considerations may conflict with each other. If they do, a government will have to make a policy choice and set priorities. A well-known example is the granting of licences to export, for example weapons or other strategic items, to a state where human rights are being violated. Which consideration should prevail? *National security?* The country in question may be an important link in the international security network. *Economic policy?* It may be essential for the survival of an important segment of national industry to be allowed to export the goods. Indeed, as it is often argued in such cases, 'if *we* don't deliver the goods, some other country will be quite willing to take our place'. *Full employment?* The industry in question may be vital for the maintenance of full employment and thus it would be suicidal from the point of view of the national interest to refuse such permission. Indeed, the labour movement is often faced with such dilemmas; on the one hand it may be quite willing to make the case for human rights, while at the same time it will be reluctant to risk losing vital employment opportunities. *Effectiveness?* On top of all that, there is no guarantee that refusal of permission to grant the requested licence will indeed help the cause of human rights. It may hurt national security, economic interests and full employment without actually achieving the desired improvement of human rights. Thus a negative decision on the requested export licence may be quite costly in those other policy areas and in the end it may merely result in the good feeling of 'having done something'. That may be a pleasant feeling for a private citizen, from a moral point of view.

However, as important as moral views are, they are not the only considerations that should guide foreign policy. A government will thus be faced with difficult policy decisions, especially where human rights considerations are involved.

THE KIND OF POLICY CHOICES

These policy choices may involve issues that are politically of a highly sensitive nature. Should a donor country use development assistance to influence human rights policy in an aid-receiving country? Should development aid to a country where human rights are systematically violated be cut off? Will this help? Such questions may on occasion lead to heated political debates in parliament pressing cabinet ministers to come up with a systematic and satisfactory answer. Yet governments find it hard to come up with such systematic answers. 'Such issues should be decided on a case-by-case basis' is an often heard but hardly very satisfactory response.

Another policy choice is that of deciding which countries to concentrate on. Should a government direct its concern for human rights to countries of whatever political colour? In other words, should it be 'non-partisan' and 'non-selective'? Should a human rights policy be 'even-handed' or is that not necessary? Should a government see it as a problem if it is being accused of 'selective indignation'? Should it be allowed to make human rights policy an instrument of security policy, so that attention is concentrated only on countries that are already or may become its enemies? Or should it rather focus on countries that belong to its own political and cultural sphere? A matter for consideration may be which policy is thought to be most effective. The government of the Netherlands once noted that 'there is more reason to make our views known in cases which concern the observance of human rights in the Western countries with which the Netherlands has close, cultural and political ties'.[1] That is a very principled and attractive sounding point of departure, but the question is whether such an approach can be maintained in political practice. Criticism of the human rights performance of one's allies may be misused by one's enemies. On the whole, governments will therefore be reluctant to pay systematically greater attention to the human rights performance of their friends than to that of their foes – at least in public. There are of course always informal channels, as part of what is often called 'silent diplomacy', through which one can, away from the public ear, express one's views.

DILEMMAS

Having to make difficult choices and setting of priorities is of course part of *all* policy-making, but it is more problematic in the field of human rights than in other areas. First of all, human rights policy may conflict with the maintenance of friendly relations with foreign governments. This is of course especially the case if the foreign government in question is responsible for gross human rights violations. That will call for a response by those governments which emphasize human rights as an element of their foreign policy. Their embassies will be instructed to report on the human rights situation, if necessary on the basis of some specific fact-finding, which may involve asking questions that may be perceived as unfriendly by the offending government. The latter may even see this as endangering mutual friendly relations. Obviously, these relations could be even further endangered if the questions are followed up by criticism, especially if such criticism is publicly expressed.

Another factor is that human rights policy often implies that a government deals with matters that other governments consider as their 'domestic affairs'. This means a choice between respecting traditional sovereignty and interference in 'somebody else's affairs'. For many years, the government of the Republic of South Africa claimed that apartheid was a purely domestic matter with which on the basis of article 2, paragraph 7 of the Charter of the United Nations, the outside world, and the United Nations in particular, had no business. Eventually, the Security Council acted on the grounds that the situation in South Africa, if unchanged, might endanger international peace and security. The government of South Africa is of course not the only one that has tried to hide its violations of human rights under the domestic jurisdiction provision of the Charter. Governments prefer to keep their human rights violations secret, or, if such efforts are unsuccessful, to claim that it is no business of the international community. The international community, for its part, will point to the seriousness of the violations in question, disregarding the domestic jurisdiction argument. Resolutions of UN bodies and other international organizations are often cited in support. Thus it is reasoned, for instance, that the right to life is of such a fundamental nature that it should be considered more important than national sovereignty. That can be seen as an important factor to support interference by international organizations, such as the United Nations. Later in this volume we shall deal with the question of whether this might also lead to unilateral intervention by other states, of a military or non-military nature (see Chapter 4).

COORDINATION OF HUMAN RIGHTS POLICY

A well-organized system of policy coordination at governmental level can greatly facilitate the making of policy choices. Thus in some countries there exists a coordination mechanism *within* the Ministry of Foreign Affairs that deals with human rights matters. The various divisions and sections within the Ministry will offer their views, often by way of commenting on a draft policy paper before a decision is taken at higher level. What is often lacking, however, is sufficient coordination *between* ministerial departments. This means that below ministerial level there may be insufficient systematic discussion of human rights as related to other policy considerations. This is especially of importance with regard to ministries dealing with subjects such as economic affairs, international trade, development assistance and defence. Of course, at the ministerial level the Minister of Foreign Affairs can always raise human rights concerns with his colleagues, but then it may often be too late. A well-balanced and thought out human rights policy should be prepared and considered by *all* departments concerned. That should help to guarantee that all major points of view are taken into consideration as well as all possible means for conducting an effective human rights policy.

It is not easy to set up a well balanced and effectively functioning interministerial coordination unit, as, apart from the Ministry of Foreign Affairs, most departments tend to pay prior attention to national considerations and national interests. They maintain close relations with specific sectors of the population and interest groups, which usually emphasize aspects other than human rights. Such interest groups often do not need to exercise undue pressure on 'their' ministry, as they already know that their views will be taken into consideration. In most countries there exist close relations between the business community and the Ministry of Economic Affairs, who influence each other. It would seem obvious that in that ministry considerations of an economic nature will prevail over human rights. What is important is that the views of these officials are challenged by those of other ministries that tend to put more emphasis on human rights considerations.

Non-governmental public interest groups in the field of human rights must primarily turn to the Ministry of Foreign Affairs. This ministry, which aims at the maintenance of coherence and consistency of foreign policy, is naturally concerned with the relations with the international community. Next to human rights it must also ensure that the country does not become internationally isolated, and will therefore try to maintain close relations with the country's geographical neighbours and with its allies. For West European countries this means maintaining close relations with the EU partners and NATO allies. In the case of human rights, special attention is being paid to what are often called the 'like-minded countries', which term usually refers to countries such as Norway, Sweden, Denmark, Canada and the Netherlands, which traditionally tend to put great emphasis on human rights in their foreign policy. The Ministry of Foreign Affairs must always consider the relative importance of emphasizing human rights as compared with the maintenance of friendly relations with all foreign governments. The position of the Ministry of Foreign Affairs varies in various countries. Where it is relatively weak, it may become involved only at a very late stage of negotiations on such issues as arms exports and other strategic trade relations. That may make it even harder to give sufficient consideration to the human rights aspects of such agreements.

PEACE AND SECURITY

Human rights will not always figure at the top of the list of priorities, even of those governments that see human rights as a central element in their foreign policy. Less will be said about human rights if the offending government happens to be a major power. Criticism of human rights policies of such countries as the United States, the former Soviet Union or China can lead to an undesirable increase of tension in the world. Former Dutch Foreign Minister Max van der Stoel, who is now serving as OSCE High Commissioner on National Minorities, and whose commitment to human rights is beyond doubt, once wrote:

> there are ... situations in which human rights policy, in my opinion, should not be given absolute priority. Would it, for example, be correct policy on the eve of an important breakthrough in arms control negotiations, to risk reaching agreement by putting forward the condition that first certain specific human rights violations should be ended? I do not think so: the interest of peace and security should prevail.[2]

Conflicts may develop between human rights and other foreign policy aims which could lead to a difficult process of weighing. Turkey is a case in point. Although for many years gross human rights violations have been taking place in Turkey, as witnessed by the reports of human rights organizations,[3] western governments have on the whole been reluctant to put more than perfunctory pressure on the Turkish government to change that situation. The state complaint under the European Convention on Human Rights by Norway, Sweden, Denmark, France and the Netherlands of 1982, led in 1985 to a friendly settlement by which Turkey committed itself to submit three reports in 1986 on the measures it had taken to ensure the prohibition of torture practices.[4] These reports have never been made public and the practice of torture has not been put to an end. The said West European governments have refrained from lodging another state complaint, and the OSCE mechanism (see Chapter 4) has not been put into action against Turkey. Other powerful western governments, such as the United States, the United Kingdom and Germany[5] have remained silent. It seems rather obvious that in the case of 'staunch NATO ally' Turkey, security interests have prevailed over human rights considerations.

4 Policy Instruments

Governments command a great number of instruments which can be used to influence other governments' policy. Such instruments vary roughly from 'making a friendly request' to military intervention. Between these two extremes lie many possibilities. The late Evan Luard, a British diplomat and scholar, has presented a list of such possibilities, which is discussed below.[1]

POSSIBILITIES

A traditional and very common possibility is to approach another government through confidential, diplomatic channels. 'Quiet diplomacy' is the classical way in which governments, through the ages, have dealt with each other.[2] It is a matter of judgement, which may differ from case to case, whether it is more effective to take up human rights matters in public or in private. Sometimes a government can more easily be persuaded to make concessions if there is no threat of loss of face involved. On other occasions, publicity, or the *threat* of such publicity, may force a government into action. Governments often *allege* that they are busy taking action through diplomatic channels, when faced with critical questions by members of parliament or journalists. For obvious reasons, such statements cannot be verified. It is a matter of faith whether or not one is prepared to believe them. If a minister has shown on other occasions that he is personally seriously concerned with human rights questions, he is more likely to be believed when referring to confidential approaches than if he is not known for his commitment to human rights. Even non-governmental organizations such as Amnesty International do not always act in public, but may prefer acts of 'quiet diplomacy'. The determining factor is what method is expected to be most effective.

A common way is to look for support among other governments. A joint démarche is usually more likely to be effective
than a solitary action. Such countries as Norway, Sweden,
Denmark, Finland, the Netherlands and Canada often find
each other to be 'like-minded' in matters of human rights.
For the Scandinavian countries, this was, for instance, the
case in joint efforts to combat apartheid in South Africa. The
Netherlands, on the other hand, has on occasion looked for
support among its European Union partners, which have
decided in principle to develop a common foreign policy.[3]
An added advantage of joint action is that a lesser burden is
placed on overall bilateral relations with governments that
are responsible for human rights violations. Thus, this type of
'burden-sharing' may be rather effective.

On the other hand, the wish to act jointly may also have
negative effects. For example, according to some experts,
the Netherlands too quickly agreed to joint withdrawal –
'friendly settlement' as it was officially worded – of the
European states' complaint against Turkey in 1985. Critics
felt at the time that the Turkish government had made little
or no commitment to improving the human rights situation
and was let off far too easily.[4] A second example is provided
by the efforts of a number of EC members, including the
Netherlands, to impose sanctions on South Africa, including an import-stop of South African coal. Germany and
Portugal, the only major European consumers of South
African coal, however, successfully opposed this proposal. In
that case, the direct economic interests of the EC member-
states clearly diverged, which made it impossible to impose
the sanctions favoured by the majority.

Public statements, in parliament or at international organizations such as the United Nations, are often also meant for
domestic consumption. Thus President Ronald Reagan on
the eve of his summit meeting with Mikhail Gorbachev in
Reykjavík in the summer of 1987, stated publicly that he intended to put strong emphasis on human rights and the improvement of the position of Soviet Jews. The final
communiqué of the meeting contains, however, little of the
sort. Reagan's announcement was evidently chiefly meant to

meet the wishes of an important segment of American public opinion. Public statements can be used to lay down a policy line to which one can refer later. At the same time, it diminishes the flexibility of a government's policy.

In organs of the United Nations a state can choose to adopt an active position, for example as a member of the Commission on Human Rights. But even if a state is not a member of that body, it is entitled to attend the meetings as an observer and make statements on human rights in general or particular issues or countries. It thus may act to promote the observance of human rights. Such promotion also takes place in the Third Committee (for social and cultural affairs) which is the sub-organ of the General Assembly where issues of human rights are discussed.

The cancellation or postponement of ministerial visits can be a manner in which to express criticism of the human rights situation in another country. The ministerial visit itself can also be used for this purpose, although this requires considerable caution, in view of the sensitivity of such issues. The host government will usually not appreciate clearly expressed criticisms of its policies on the part of a visiting foreign dignitary. Firm pronouncements may be applauded at home, but may not at all have the desired effect abroad. Such a visit, if extended to a country that is known for its poor record in human rights, must be very carefully prepared, to prevent it from being misused by the host country as a sign of approval for its policies.

Violations of human rights can lead to a restriction or breaking-off of contacts in the fields of culture or sports. Thus, for a long time many nations refused to have such contacts with South Africa, by way of protest against its policy of apartheid, in response to resolutions to that effect adopted by the General Assembly of the United Nations. On the whole, this attitude was supported by the victims of apartheid, as represented by organizations of black South Africans, such as the African National Congress.

However, with the benefit of hindsight, it is now often said that breaking off all academic contacts was not wise, as it mainly affected the opponents of apartheid, while its proponents tended to disregard UN resolutions anyway. In other cases it has been even more difficult to decide on a proper response. For example, extensive debates have dealt with the question of whether to extend expert legal training to judges, lawyers, officials and students in countries where human rights are being violated by the government. Proponents of such training projects argue that they will make legal practitioners more aware of international human rights norms, while opponents see it mainly as an indirect measure of support to the offending regime. Ceausescu's Romania was another case, where opinions abroad differed widely as to whether the maintenance of international cultural ties would help the regime to stay in power, or whether it would serve to support its opponents. In such cases both parties are aiming for the same thing: improvement of the human rights situation. They have, however, diametrically opposed views with regard to which means should be employed to achieve that aim.

SANCTIONS

The measures which have been discussed so far all belong to the realm of what may be called the friendly or 'soft' sector. Far more controversial are instruments in the category of sanctions. Governments are more reluctant to apply them, among other reasons because they may hurt themselves. An illustration is provided by the arms embargo against South Africa. Most western states were only willing to enter into such an embargo after the Security Council had taken an explicit position in support of such sanctions. Governments tend to hide behind the argument 'if we don't do it, some other country may'. Moreover, the effect of such a measure is often put into question. It might hurt the wrong persons, promote a 'lager-mentality' or be counterproductive. A similar argument was often heard against the establishment of an oil-embargo against South Africa.

    It is rather difficult to distinguish in such debates the arguments that are based on finding the most effective ways to promote human rights from those which are used for other political or economic reasons. The discussion about the effect of economic sanctions is an old one. Would an oil-embargo against South Africa in and of itself have ended apartheid? Probably not immediately, but it might have hastened the demise of the system and have brought the regime into difficulties. In the event, international disapproval undoubtedly contributed to the eventual dissolution of apartheid, but its final termination as well as what is going to succeed it, depended in the end on the people of South Africa themselves.

DEVELOPMENT AID

The instrument of a denial or cancellation of development aid was already briefly discussed in the previous chapter. In addition to the problem of 'manipulation', there is the danger that such measures may hurt the wrong people – the very poor for whom development aid was set up in the first place. Members of government, even of very poor countries, rarely suffer directly from the withholding of development aid.

It is very difficult to determine whether in the case of gross and systematic human rights violations the cancellation or suspension of development aid is or is not an effective instrument to restore human rights. The Netherlands suspended its large aid programme to its former colony Suriname in 1982, after the summary execution by the military regime of fifteen known opponents (see Chapter 11). Difficult as it is to determine *afterwards* whether the instruments employed have been effective, it is even harder to decide *beforehand*. Therefore, for donor countries, in order to avoid the charge of complicity, it must be made clear that its aid is not to be used for purposes of repression or to help the repressive regime. The only way to stay 'clean' is not to give any aid at all to countries with repressive regimes. Such a 'clean hands' policy is, however, not going to help the poor people of the world and would limit aid to the happy few human rights observing countries such as Costa Rica, Botswana and Oman. Such a policy would obviously be self-defeating. There are just no easy solutions to the problem.

One way of expressing disapproval of a recipient government's human rights record would be to cut aid programmes by a certain percentage, as Norway has done in the case of Sri Lanka. But the recipient country may retaliate by refusing aid programmes altogether, as Indonesia did in 1992 in the case of the Netherlands (see Chapter 11).

Positive sanctions may be more effective than negative ones. Development aid is after all intended to improve economic and social human rights in the recipient country. Development aid can also be used to support local institutions that try to promote civil and political rights. This may entail giving support to the judicial process, improving the role of the communication media, assisting the development of independent trade unions, giving training and refresher courses to judges, helping prison reform, designing legislation that is in accordance with international standards, giving human rights education to the military and the police, supporting relevant UN projects as well as university cooperation. Support may also be extended to local movements working on behalf of the development of democracy and the promotion of respect for human rights.[5]

DIPLOMATIC RELATIONS

Breaking off diplomatic relations is an instrument by which a government can express its disapproval of another government's policy, for example in the realm of human rights. But this instrument can be a double-edged sword. Luard has pointed to the negative aspects of breaking off diplomatic relations. He gives the example of Cambodia, where between 1975 and 1978 dreadful killings took place. As no western government maintained diplomatic relations with the country at the time, there was no possibility of even trying to influence the Cambodian government.

Moreover, little was known outside Cambodia of what was happening there. A similar example was the situation in the African state Equatorial Guinea under the equally isolated Nguema regime, which was also guilty of gross and systematic human rights violations. Luard is strongly opposed to the breaking-off of diplomatic relations with this type of regime:

> There is a double disadvantage in such situations. On the one hand, there is little external influence on the government concerned. On the other hand, the oppressed population feels deserted and without recourse. Potential centres of resistance lose hope. Churches and religious groups, without support from elsewhere, lose influence. A policy of isolating a country where such events are taking place is thus the opposite of what in fact is required.[6]

One might add that in many Latin American countries foreign embassies have often functioned as a refuge for political opponents of local repressive regimes. In communist East Europe western embassies gave moral and material support to dissident movements. These are additional reasons to maintain diplomatic representations in such countries. If one accepts these arguments, then the signals of disapproval which are expressed by breaking off diplomatic relations must be abandoned. It means, however, that the diplomatic representatives should be clearly instructed as to which activities *vis-à-vis* the oppressive government they should take part in, and which not.

INTERVENTION

The strongest and most drastic instrument governments use to put pressure on other governments is intervention, if need be military intervention. Intervention is some manner of forceful interference by a state in the domestic or foreign affairs of another state, in order to bring about a certain kind of behaviour by that other state. Such use of force is not permitted under the rules of international law. This has, for example, been clearly formulated in the Declaration on Principles of International Law concerning Friendly Relations and Co-operation among States in accordance with the Charter of the United Nations, which was adopted by the General Assembly of the United Nations in 1970:[7]

> Every State has the duty to refrain in its international relations from the threat or use of force against the territorial integrity or political independence of any State, or in any manner inconsistent with the purposes of the United Nations.

The prohibition of the use of force also extends to what is known as 'humanitarian intervention', which refers to the unilateral threat or use of armed force by one state against another to protect the life and liberty of nationals of the latter from acts or omissions by their own government.[8] There has been a continuing debate on the question of whether gross and systematic violations of human rights in a country entitle foreign governments to resort to military intervention to put an end of such violations. The widespread occurrence of violations of human rights in countries such as Iraq, the former Yugoslavia, Somalia and Liberia have given new impetus to this debate. Some argue that military intervention is only permitted if sanctioned by the UN Security Council. Yet interpretations differ widely as to under what circumstances the Council is authorized to take that decision. Under the present Charter provisions, the Council can only act in the case of a threat to international peace and security. Gross human rights violations, while threatening life and liberty of the local population, do not necessarily pose a threat to international peace and security. Should the international community nevertheless be entitled to intervene militarily? This would clearly run counter to the concept of national sovereignty, which lies at the basis of traditional international relations and which is enshrined in article 2(7) of the Charter of the United Nations ('Nothing contained in the present Charter shall authorise the United Nations to intervene in matters which are essentially within the domestic jurisdiction of any state'). An additional difficulty is how to define precisely under what circumstances such military intervention would be allowed and how to prevent states from abusing it for political ends of their own. Even limited actions, such as the creation of 'safe havens' for the Kurdish population in the north of Iraq by joint United States–British–Italian–Dutch action in 1991, which was explicitly rejected by the government of Iraq, are based on questionable legal grounds.[9] In its resolutions on the oppression of the Kurds in Iraq[10] and on Somalia[11] the Security Council established a direct link between gross violations of fundamental human rights and the existence of a threat to international peace and security. In the resolution on the Kurds the Security Council condemned the repression of the Iraqi civilian population in many parts of Iraq, including most recently the Kurdish-populated areas, '*the consequences of which threaten international peace and security in the region*' (italic added). It 'insisted' that Iraq should allow immediate access by international humanitarian organizations to all those in need of assistance in all parts of Iraq. But so far it has never explicitly sanctioned military intervention to combat human rights violations. Next to the legal complexity of the issue, there is the practical problem that it may be relatively easy to decide when to intervene, but far more difficult to determine when the task has been accomplished and the troops can leave again.

History is full of examples of unilateral military intervention, often with the announced intention to 'restore law and order'. In this century, the United States intervened many times in Central America and the Caribbean, most recently in Grenada (1983) and in Panama (1989); the Soviet Union in Hungary (1956), in Czechoslovakia (1968) and in Afghanistan (1979). In some instances such as in Hungary, intervention took place at the 'invitation' of a local government that was in trouble; in such cases the prohibition of intervention under international law was by-passed. None of these interventions took place for the real or ostensible reason of defending human rights.

Even more pertinent to the present context are the military interventions by Asian and African states, which at first sight appear to have occurred in reaction to human rights violations. The first of these was the military intervention by India in East Pakistan in 1971, which ended the slaughter of Bengali citizens by the Pakistan army and resulted in the proclamation of the independent state of Bangladesh. The second was the invasion by Tanzania in Uganda in 1979, terminating the murderous rule of dictator Idi Amin. Finally, there was the occupation of Cambodia by Vietnam in 1979, which overthrew the even more murderous rule of the *Khmers Rouges* of Pol Pot. None of the intervening states based their actions on humanitarian or human rights considerations. India justified its attack by alleging that it had first been attacked by Pakistan; Tanzania claimed that its troops had invaded Uganda to punish Amin for an earlier raid into Tanzania – its invasion allegedly coincided with a domestic revolt in Uganda against Amin; Vietnam denied at first that its troops had invaded Cambodia and claimed that Pol Pot had been deposed by the Cambodians themselves.[12] The reason for these denials is obvious: to recognize the legitimacy of humanitarian intervention would create a precedent which at some other point in time could be used against the intervening state. Thus Pakistan might use it to legitimize attacking India for its treatment of its Moslim subjects or China might invade Vietnam for its treatment of its Chinese minority population.

In the way they justified their actions, the three states – India, Tanzania and Vietnam – conformed to existing practice. In the course of history the principle of non-intervention has been accepted as serving the interests of all states, because it removes a source of possible conflicts and contributes thereby to the maintenance of international order and stability – in the sense of maintaining the status quo.

The former Soviet Union, like most other states, has always defended the principle of non-intervention in the affairs of other states, although it did not always practise what it preached. It is was one of the reasons why in 1948 it abstained in the vote in the General Assembly on the

Universal Declaration of Human Rights. In the Soviet view, international cooperation in the field of human rights should go together with respect for the sovereign equality of all states and non-interference in affairs that belong to the domestic jurisdiction of states. However, the Soviet Union used to argue that only under exceptional circumstances may states intervene in the affairs of other states. These circumstances occur in the case of aggression, fascism, national-socialism, colonialism, apartheid and racism. These serious and systematic violations of human rights may threaten world peace and should be fought. Most western governments, on the other hand, tend to claim that human rights do not belong to 'domestic affairs' and that at least non-violent external interference is definitely justified. Such interference is distinguished from military intervention and may consist of exerting pressure by diplomatic means or through the use of radio broadcasts.[13]

APARTHEID

In the case of South Africa's policy of apartheid, the UN has legitimized its actions by referring to the threat it posed to international peace and security. As early as 1960, the Security Council declared that the situation in South Africa had led to international friction which, if it continued, might threaten international peace and security. In 1972, the Council expressed its concern that the situation in South Africa disturbed international peace and security in southern Africa. Eventually, the Security Council decided on a mandatory arms embargo, prohibiting any state from providing South Africa with arms and military equipment for police use. It also banned cooperation with South Africa in nuclear development. After the killing of hundreds of people by the police in the black township of Soweto in 1976, the Security Council condemned the South African government and called on it to end apartheid because of its effects on peace.

Since then, the Council has become involved in the matter of South African raids on its neighbouring countries, issuing condemnations and warnings. But it has never adopted proposals for stronger economic and military sanctions, because the western countries declined to support such actions. The Soviet Union used to verbally support coercion, but it never made more concrete commitments, although it gave substantial covert aid to liberation movements. The General Assembly also yearly adopted a series of resolutions condemning apartheid.

South Africa, for its part, always claimed that this type of resolution interfered in its domestic affairs, which meant a violation of article 2(7) of the UN Charter. Was apartheid in its heyday a threat to international peace and security? Yes, if it meant that South Africa – as it did on several occasions – let apartheid go together with military attacks on its neighbours. But was apartheid also a threat to international peace and security in the absence of such attacks? Strictly speaking one could argue that a repressive regime that stays within its own borders does not pose a threat to *international* peace and security. That is only the case if it crosses its borders and tries to impose its policy on other countries as well.

In the case of the South African policy of apartheid a much stronger line of reasoning is that states are legally bound to higher obligations than just refraining from interference in each other's domestic affairs. R.J. Vincent has expressed this reasoning in the following terms:

> [W]hen a state by its behaviour so outrages the conscience of mankind, no doctrine can be deployed to defend it against intervention. Thus it might be argued that states had not only a right but a duty to overrule the principle of non-intervention in order to defend the Jews against Nazi persecution and a parallel is drawn and similar argument urged in support of intervention against the institution of *apartheid* in present-day South Africa.[14]

The logic of his argument leads to the conclusion that states that violate internationally accepted legally binding standards cannot appeal to the principle of non-interference.[15] Apartheid was undoubtedly a flagrant violation of fundamental human rights, as codified in the Universal

Declaration of Human Rights, the two UN covenants of 1966 and a large number of international treaties. Such a flagrant violation justifies external interference, even if it belongs, as the South African government used to claim, basically to 'domestic affairs'.

THE HELSINKI CONFERENCE

The dilemma between the need for effective instruments to protect human rights versus the principle of non-interference is reflected in the Final Act of the Helsinki Conference on Security and Cooperation in Europe (CSCE) of 1975. This Final Act, which was originally signed by all European states except Albania, plus the United States and Canada, and which now is adhered to by 53 states including Albania and all successor states to the Soviet Union, contains two principles which at first sight seem to contradict each other. The sixth principle deals with non-intervention in internal affairs:

> The participating States will refrain from any intervention, direct or indirect, individual or collective, in the internal or external affairs falling within the domestic jurisdiction of another participating State, regardless of their mutual relations.

This would mean that supervision over human rights would be left to every state itself. Human rights are mentioned in the seventh principle that deals with respect for human rights and fundamental freedoms, including the freedom of thought, conscience, religion or belief:

> The participating States will respect human rights and fundamental freedoms, including the freedom of thought, conscience, religion or belief, for all without distinction as to race, sex, language or religion.

No rank order was established among the principles. The Helsinki Final Act even explicitly excludes such a rank order:

All the principles set forth above are of primary significance and, accordingly, they will be equally and unreservedly applied, each of them being interpreted taking into account the others.

The human rights paragraphs in the Final Act gained considerably in importance when dissident groups in the Soviet Union and other East European countries began to use these texts to call their own governments to account over their violations of human rights. 'Helsinki monitoring groups', including 'Charter 77' in Czechoslovakia, were established, which aimed at supervising their governments in this respect. The activities of these groups were greatly hindered by the governments; many of their members were arrested. Under the regime of Leonid Brezhnev in the Soviet Union most of these groups were forced to stop their activities.

If intervention takes place through the use of non-violent means, this would mean that the sixth principle of the Helsinki Final Act cannot be used to prevent other countries from commenting on the lack of implementation of the human rights provisions that are mentioned in the seventh principle. This interpretation was, however, never accepted by the communist states of Eastern Europe. It would then be correct to describe the conflicts about human rights matters, at the time of the East–West struggle, as 'an essay on the rival claims of Principle VI and Principle VII'.[16]

The Concluding Document of the CSCE follow-up meeting in Vienna, which was approved in January 1989, contained numerous detailed provisions on human rights. Thus the participating states recognized, among others, the freedom to leave one's country and to return to it, as well as the freedom of religion. They endeavoured to protect the identity of minorities and to improve the working freedom of journalists. From now on, the CSCE commitments concerning respect for all human rights and fundamental freedoms, human contacts and other issues of a related humanitarian character were to be known as the 'human dimension' of CSCE. A new mechanism was developed to handle specific violations within the human dimension. This mechanism contained the following provisions:

- participating States are obliged to react to requests for information about the human dimension by other participating States;
- they must be willing to hold bilateral meetings about such issues;
- each participating State is entitled to inform all other participating States about the questions concerned;
- finally, participating States are entitled to raise such issues at the annual conferences on the human dimension and the next CSCE follow-up meeting.

These provisions were further elaborated and refined at the meetings on the human dimension, held in Paris (1989), Copenhagen (1990) and Moscow (1991) and at the follow-up meeting in Helsinki (1992). In Helsinki it was decided to continue to hold annual implementation meetings on human dimension issues. The main task of these meetings will be to review implementation of all CSCE human dimension commitments, while indirectly a further development of these commitments is also provided for.[17]

CONSISTENCY

It is often claimed that governments should pursue a certain degree of consistency in their choice of instruments to promote human rights. This means that in equal situations equal means should be employed. It is commonly assumed that governments will be more persuasive if they react equally to human rights violations in different political settings. Evan Luard was a strong proponent of such consistency:

> If western governments ... denounced only human rights violations in Eastern Europe, but ignore those in the

West; if communist states denounced only the situation in Chile or Northern Ireland but say nothing of that in Cuba or Ethiopia, they cannot expect to be treated as unbiased in such campaigns.[18]

The Dutch government has often been accused of inconsistency, because it suspended its development aid to Suriname after the political murders there in 1982, but in the case of Indonesia, where equally serious human rights violations had taken place, for many years it refused to do the same. It always denied that its policy had been inconsistent in view of the major differences in the aid-receiving countries. It seems, however, that the Dutch government more strongly emphasized the notions of 'complicity' and 'regime-support' in the case of Suriname than in the case of Indonesia. In the latter case, other western donor countries were willing to take over the role of the Dutch. While this policy can be understood as realistic, its lack of consistency may damage the credibility of overall human rights policy.

Absolute consistency is not necessarily always most effective. Former British Foreign Minister, David Owen, relates that when he made human rights a major item of his foreign policy he warned that its price might be a little inconsistency. On second thoughts, he writes, it was not a matter of a little inconsistency, but a great deal of inconsistency. He does not seem to regret this.[19] Assuming that international standards should always be equally applied, an effective foreign policy can nevertheless imply that in similar situations different instruments are employed. However, the burden of proof that an inconsistent or less consistent policy may be more effective in the promotion of human rights, rests with the government choosing such instruments.

CONCLUSION

The instruments that are available for the promotion of human rights do not differ fundamentally from those

serving other aspects of foreign policy. An important crite-
rion in the selection of policy instruments is their expected
effectiveness. Small and medium-sized states may find it
useful to tune their policy to that of the 'like-minded'. The
voice of two, three or fifteen (the EU!) states will be more
influential than the voice of one. However, this may raise
the difficulty of reaching agreement among sovereign units
and the chance that the original point of view my become
diluted. In addition, the decision-making process consisting
of numerous rounds of negotiations is almost unverifiable.
This may again negatively affect the credibility of policies.
Difficult choices have to be made between effectiveness,
credibility and the necessity of looking for compromises.

Finally, there is the matter of credibility to a government's own domestic public. Foreign policy is not made *in
vacuo*. Foreign policy makers must take account of domestic
public opinion. That public opinion is expressed in parliament, in the press, through political parties and by non-
governmental organizations. Violations of human rights in
other parts of the world are reported in the media and may
elicit indignant reactions. This is another aspect which
governments have to consider in their choice of policy
instruments.

5 Domestic Sources of Foreign Policy

Foreign policy is not made *in vacuo*. It is the result of an influencing process that consists of many external as well as internal factors. This chapter deals with internal factors, in particular parliament and non-governmental organizations.

PARLIAMENT

It is difficult to make general observations about the role of national parliaments in foreign policy making with particular reference to human rights. That role can differ considerably, depending on the national context. Below is shown, with the help of a number of examples, what parliaments can do in this field. Attention is focused on parliaments of the western-democratic type, as these would seem to play a more important role than parliaments in a non-western context.

It should be emphasized from the beginning that the role of parliament in this field is only an aspect of the role of parliament in overall foreign policy. That role is of a limited nature. Some experts think that parliaments *cannot* play a significant role in foreign policy making; others think that they *ought not* to play such a role. Attention has been called to such factors as the importance of continuity, consistency, coherence and secrecy in foreign policy, which could be endangered by too large an involvement of parliament.

The constitutional role of the legislature with regard to foreign policy in most parliamentary systems is no different from that in domestic policy. It consists mainly of control over the budget, legislation and overall policy control, which in most West European political systems – as differing from a presidential system like that of the United States – is

49

expressed through ministerial accountability: cabinet ministers occupy their positions as long as they have the
confidence of a majority of parliament.

On the whole, there is not a great amount of national legislation enacted in the field of foreign policy. There are of
course international bilateral or multilateral treaties which
require parliamentary approval. In the United States this
right is reserved to the Senate. This body can also in other
ways play an important role in foreign policy because of its
role in the approval of appointment of ministers and senior
civil servants, including ambassadors.

In general, parliamentary control over foreign policy, including human rights policy, takes place *afterwards*, when
the minister concerned must account for his conduct of
policy. It is much more difficult for parliament to give the
minister specific instructions *beforehand*. The minister will –
with some justification – argue that he needs some freedom
of action in his negotiations with other governments. A
minister who can only act under detailed instructions
from parliament will have a difficult task in international
negotiations, which consist in great part of seeking viable
compromises.

The absence of control beforehand is somewhat counter-
balanced by parliament's right to put questions to ministers.
Members of parliament can thus direct the attention of the
government to the human rights situation in specific countries. They acquire their information often with the help of
non-governmental organizations (see below). Human rights
are a subject where extra-parliamentary activities can
strengthen the role of parliament. This may happen in a
rather informal way. It can also happen in the form of *public
hearings* which have been mainly developed in the United
States and which have been adopted by many other parliaments. During such hearings individual experts and representatives of non-governmental organizations can put
forward their views.

In some countries efforts have been made to put contacts
between parliamentarians and one particular non-governmental organization – Amnesty International – on a formal

footing by the holding of periodic meetings. These meetings usually lapse after a while, however, because parliamentarians are busy people who at the last minute may be called away to attend other business. Only in Australia has such an effort apparently been more of a permanent success. Some twenty senators, more than forty members of the House of Representatives and about twenty staff members belong to a group called 'Parliamentarians for Amnesty'. This group meets on a regular basis. It handles so-called 'urgent actions', drawn up by Amnesty International in cases of torture, extrajudicial executions, disappearances and the death penalty. According to its own report, this group is rather active and somewhat successful in stimulating the Australian government to take action in the case of human rights violations.

In most parliamentary democracies the presentation of the budget of the Ministry of Foreign Affairs is the yearly occasion to discuss, among others, human rights matters. The members of parliament make use of comments and information often supplied by non-governmental human rights organizations. That is also the moment to examine the conduct of the government in organs of international organizations, such as the General Assembly of the United Nations and the UN Commission on Human Rights.

Foreign visits by parliamentary delegations can be used to discuss gross violations of human rights. The members of parliament must be well informed before they start on such trips, know what they want to see, which people they want to talk to, etc. Otherwise there is always the danger that the visit will be abused by the regime in question and be interpreted as support for its policies. In this connection it may be useful to demand that independent journalists or academics be asked to accompany the tour.

On the whole, national legislation does not play a major role in the area of foreign policy. There are, however, exceptions to this general rule. The United States Congress has, for instance, adopted legislation dealing with the relationship between foreign aid and human rights performance. Section 116 of the Foreign Assistance Act prohibits giving assistance to the government of any country that engages in a consistent pattern of gross violations of internationally recognized human rights, unless such assistance will directly benefit the needy people in such a country. Section 502B of the same act states that no security assistance may be provided to any country whose government engages in a consistent pattern of gross violations of internationally recognized human rights. The State Department must annually report on the human rights situation in each country proposed as a recipient of security assistance. These reports, which now cover all countries in the world, together with the critical comments by human rights organizations, provide an important source of information about the situation with regard to civil and political rights in these countries. The International Financial Institutions Act of 1977 provides that the United States government must oppose loans to gross violators of human rights, unless such assistance is directed specifically to programmes which serve the basic needs of the citizens of such countries.[1]

The Norwegian Parliament decided in the period 1984–6 that the government should financially support independent institutions that issue annual reports about the human rights situation in countries that receive Norwegian development assistance.[2] The Norwegian government showed at first little enthusiasm for the idea, but had to accept the decision of the parliament. These reports, the first of which were prepared by two Norwegian research institutes, received an international dimension in 1988 when the Danish Centre for Human Rights jointed the operation.[3] The 1989, 1990, 1991 and 1993 reports were prepared by the same institutes, joined by research institutes in Sweden, Finland, Canada, Austria and the Netherlands.[4]

The Netherlands Parliament asked the government in 1979 for a high-level human rights officer. This led to the appointment of a coordinator and a deputy-coordinator for human rights in the Ministry of Foreign Affairs. The Parliament was also instrumental in the reactivation of the defunct Advisory Council on Human Rights and Foreign Policy. This Committee that consists of non-governmental experts, advises the Minister of Foreign Affairs at his request or on its own initiative on questions of human rights in foreign policy (see Chapter 11).

NON-GOVERNMENTAL ORGANIZATIONS

Non-governmental organizations monitor the observance of human rights, publish violations of human rights, collect information and work for the benefit of victims. These organizations control their own finances, personnel and policy and operate independently of governments. They receive little or no financial support from governments and operate both within the territory of national states and internationally. Some of them are international federations of national organizations, while others are organized internationally with national sections in the different countries.

In the field of human rights at least three types of non-governmental organizations can be distinguished:[5]

(a) general non-governmental organizations which occasionally deal with human rights, versus organizations that only deal with human rights;
(b) global versus regional organizations;
(c) permanent versus ad hoc organizations.

(a) The *churches* are first and foremost among general non-governmental organizations which also concern themselves with human rights. Many churches are members of the World Council of Churches, which at times expresses views about human rights violations. So do individual church leaders, for instance in the past in the matter of South Africa's apartheid policies. They have also given support to anti-apartheid organizations.

Another type of body that does not specialize in human rights, but sometimes takes positions on them, are *professional organizations* that may undertake actions on behalf of persecuted colleagues in other countries or engage themselves in the development of professional codes of ethics.

An example of this type is the World Organization of Psychiatrists that carried out a campaign against the confinement of political dissidents in psychiatric institutions in the former Soviet Union. This led to the departure of the association of Soviet psychiatrists from the world organization. By 1989 the situation had, however, improved so much that the Soviet organization was re-admitted to the world organization.

The international association of medical doctors, the World Medical Congress, adopted a professional code a few years ago that prohibited doctors from taking part in torture practices. That is of particular importance in countries where doctors are forced to lend a helping hand in such practices. For those who are courageous enough to refuse, it is of great importance to be able to count on the support of professional colleagues elsewhere in the world.

Organizations of jurists and defence lawyers stand up for the rights of their colleagues to freely exercise their profession, for instance to defend political opponents of an oppressive regime. Organizations of journalists stand up for the right of their colleagues living under dictatorships to write and publish freely and act for the release of detained journalists. The role of trade unions is also of great importance, who appeal for the release of detained labour leaders and for the right of workers to establish free, independent trade unions that are not led by government officials. Organizations of policemen engage in the development of professional codes to prevent their colleagues from becoming engaged in torture practices.

Such activities of professional organizations are very important. They have a direct interest in expressing feelings of solidarity with their oppressed colleagues, in setting up professional codes of ethics, in standing up for colleagues that are being tortured, have 'disappeared', have been put in preventive detention, confined in psychiatric institutions, refused emigration or persecuted in other ways. Whenever necessary these organizations may ask governments for support in their activities and exert pressure on other regimes that violate human rights.

Then there are organizations that engage themselves exclusively or predominantly in matters of human rights. Such human rights organizations are Amnesty International, the International Commission of Jurists, the 'watch' committees (Human Rights Watch: Helsinki, Asia, Africa and the Americas), Justice and Peace, the Anti-Slavery Society, Article 19, the Minority Rights Group and the International League for Human Rights. These organizations do not necessarily work for *all* human rights. Amnesty International, for example, has a limited mandate. It limits its activities to the following:

- free all prisoners of conscience: these are people detained anywhere for their beliefs or because of their ethnic origin, sex, colour or language – who have not used or advocated violence;
- abolish the death penalty, torture and other cruel treatment of prisoners;
- end extrajudicial executions and 'disappearances'.[6]

(b) The work of Amnesty International and the International Commission of Jurists is of a *global* character: in principle no country in the world is excluded from their activities. The most recent annual report of Amnesty International listed no less than 151 countries in which human rights within Amnesty's concerns were being violated.[7]

Other organizations monitor geographically restricted areas. They may either focus on human rights or concern themselves more marginally with human rights. Well-known examples are the numerous national committees that deal or used to deal with such countries as Afghanistan, Chile, China, Cuba, El Salvador, Guatemala, Indonesia, Iran, Iraq, Nicaragua and South Africa.

General human rights organizations cooperate closely with such specialized geographical committees to obtain reliable and up to date information.

(c) Most of the organizations mentioned so far are of a more or less permanent nature. At times, organizations may be set up for *ad hoc* purposes, to achieve a specified limited goal; in the past, for example, international committees were established to work for the release of some specific Soviet dissidents. If the goal has been achieved within a reasonable time, the committee is formally dissolved. A good example was the organization that drew attention to violations of human rights in the Soviet Union at the preparation of and during the Olympic Games in Moscow in 1980. When the games were over, the organization was dissolved. If such an *ad hoc* organization is not successful, its activities may gradually drop off.

There usually exists a close cooperation between this type of organization and more permanent human rights organizations. The *ad hoc* organizations may be able to mobilize more attention, people and funds for a limited time, while the permanent organizations are better suited to engage in long-term activities.

SPECIFIC FUNCTIONS

Activities on behalf of human rights by non-governmental organizations include the following specific functions:

(1) the collection and distribution of information;
(2) lending legal and moral support to victims;
(3) lobbying of governments;
(4) mobilizing public opinion.

(1) The collection and distribution of reliable information may well be the most important function of non-governmental organizations in the field of human rights. Governments that are engaged in violations of human rights have an interest in keeping such activities hidden from the public view, especially as all governments tend to pay lip-service to human rights. No government will easily admit that it is engaged in torture or detains opponents without form of trial. On the contrary, governments are usually embarassed when confronted with such practices and try either to deny their existence or put forward 'mitigating circumstances'. An

organization such as Amnesty International strongly emphasizes the collection of accurate information; its effectiveness greatly depends on the veracity of its reports. It has an international secretariat in London, where a staff of almost 300 people is permanently engaged in checking and double-checking the information it receives.

The manner in which the information is collected can differ widely. In the case of Amnesty International, the personal contacts of its researchers are vital. The protection of confidential sources is essential; the most important information is stored in the heads of the researchers who may be reluctant to share it even with their immediate colleagues. This informative role of non-governmental organization is crucial because it is only rarely performed by other organizations. The effectiveness of non-governmental organizations in influencing public opinion and government officials greatly depends on their reputation for accuracy. At the stage that the information is considered ripe for publication, it may be sent for comment to the government in question; its reaction – if any – may be incorporated in the final report. It may even lead to a revision of the draft report.

When the information is available, a decision must be taken on the way of distributing it. It may become part of periodic reports, such as the series of the Minority Rights Group in London, the *Review* of the International Commission of Jurists or the special reports and the annual report of Amnesty International. It may also take the form of so-called 'urgent actions', asking people to appeal to governmental authorities to act in specific cases. It may also take the form of a press release or a press conference, a contribution to a parliamentary hearing in either written or oral form or in communications to governments or inter-governmental organizations. The purpose is always the same – 'our weapon is the mobilization of shame', says Amnesty International – though the form in which the concern is expressed may differ.

(2) Lending juridical and moral support to victims of human rights violations can mean the dispatch of lawyers and other trained observers to attend trials or the collection

of funds for the defence of victims of human rights violations and for the relief of their families, especially in the
case of vaguely described offences such as 'conspiracy
against the State', 'agitation', 'offending the State', 'social
parasitism' and the like – terms which were widely used in
the former Soviet Union.

The importance of giving moral support to prisoners
should not be underestimated. Amnesty International has
instigated the practice of 'adopting' prisoners of conscience, who are sent letters and packages and given all
sorts of support by Amnesty groups all over the world.

(3–4) Non-governmental organizations may also con-
fidentially approach governments on behalf of certain
specific cases, It can be useful to combine such a confidential approach with the announcement that certain
information will be made public *unless* the offending government is willing to engage in reforms, release political
prisoners, put an end to torture practices, etc. If this
method is not successful, the government can be asked to
admit observers to engage in fact-finding or to attend trials
of political prisoners. What remains in the last resort is publicity in order to try to change the government's views by
public pressure. Chances of success are greater if the
country concerned traditionally pays attention to expressions of public opinion. It may also lead to the exertion of
external pressure by other governments or intergovernmental organizations.

Non-governmental organizations play an important role
within intergovernmental organizations. Some of them have
observer status in organs of the United Nations and may
take part in the annual debates in the UN Commission on
Human Rights. They contribute by written and oral interventions and may submit draft texts, which may be incorporated in UN resolutions and international treaties. Back in
1973, Amnesty International organized an international
conference on torture in Paris which greatly helped to put
this issue on the international agenda. The Dutch government, which together with Sweden was instrumental in the
adoption of the international convention against torture in

1984, sent one of its top civil servants to the headquarters of Amnesty International in London when that organization expressed too many reservations with regard to the proposed draft convention. It illustrates the importance governments attach to the views of certain non-governmental organizations.[8] The Dutch and British governments send the annual reports of Amnesty International for comment to their diplomatic missions abroad.

It is difficult to measure the precise effect of the activities of non-governmental organizations in the field of human rights. It is impossible to determine whether those activities have led to fewer violations of human rights than in the past. At first sight the opposite seems to be true: the volume of the annual reports of Amnesty International and other human rights organizations is increasing and each year more countries are mentioned where human rights violations are taking place. However, an important function of these organizations is, as we saw before, the collection of information. Thus the only thing that is certain is that the quantity of *information* about human rights violations has increased over the years, which is not the same as saying that there has been an increase in the actual number of violations. The collection and distribution of information is an important factor in the struggle for improvement of the human rights situation in the world. Where states and intergovernmental organizations fail to act, non-governmental organizations play an important role in supervising respect for human rights.

6 Intergovernmental Organizations[1]

Major aspects of a state's human rights policy are developed within the framework of intergovernmental organizations. They offer an opportunity to governments, often in cooperation with other like-minded states, to raise issues of human rights. They also offer an opportunity to call states to account that are guilty of human rights violations.

The activities of intergovernmental organizations can roughly be divided into two categories: standard-setting and implementation. Most of this chapter deals with implementation as an aspect of human rights foreign policy making.

STANDARD-SETTING

International standards are contained in many international treaties and declarations that prescribe how states should behave with reference to respect for human rights. Many of these were established within the framework of the United Nations – for example, the Universal Declaration of Human Rights (1948) and the two covenants of 1966: the International Covenant on Civil and Political Rights (ICCPR) and the International Covenant on Economic, Social and Cultural Rights (ICESCR). In addition, there are numerous legally binding treaties relating to more specific rights. Some of the more important of these are: the slavery convention (1926), the convention on genocide (1948), the convention on the elimination of racial discrimination (1965), the convention against apartheid (1973), the convention against discrimination of women (1979), the anti-torture convention (1984), the body of principles for the protection of detainees (1988), the convention on the rights of the child (1989), the convention on the rights of migrant workers (1990), the declaration on minorities (1992) and the declaration on disappearances (1992). Under preparation are declarations on indigenous peoples and on human rights defenders.

Some of the specialized agencies of the United Nations have also adopted conventions and recommendations relating to human rights. UNESCO and in particular the International Labour Organisation (ILO) have been active in this field. Some of the more important conventions are the following:

- freedom of association and protection of the right to organize (ILO, 1948);
- equal remuneration for men and women for work of equal value (ILO, 1951);
- abolition of forced labour (ILO, 1930, 1957);
- discrimination in respect of employment and occupation (ILO, 1958);
- discrimination in education (UNESCO, 1960);
- employment policy (ILO, 1966);
- protection of workers' representatives (ILO, 1971);
- protection of the right to organize and procedures for determining conditions of employment in the public service (ILO, 1978);
- the right to self-determination of indigenous peoples (ILO, 1957 and 1989).

These conventions also involve supervision of national behaviour by relevant international bodies. Especially in the case of ILO, violations can lead to embarrassing publicity and even painful sanctions.

IMPLEMENTATION

Less progress has been made with the implementation than with the formulation of international human rights standards. Below, a survey is given of the most important international bodies that are engaged in the implementation of the said norms. These include the UN Commission on Human Rights and its Sub-Commission which stem directly from the UN Charter on the one hand, and organs that are based on arrangements in more specific human rights treaties on the other.

UN Commission on Human Rights

The Commission on Human Rights is the major UN organ that deals with implementation of human rights norms. It meets annually for five or six weeks.[2] Enlarged over the years, it now includes representatives of fifty-three states, elected for three-year terms by the Economic and Social Council (ECOSOC). It has a broad mandate touching on any matter relating to human rights.[3] The Commission orders and examines studies, usually drafted by rapporteurs or by the Human Rights Centre in Geneva, which is a division of the UN Secretariat. It drafts international treaties relating to human rights for adoption by the General Assembly and thereupon for ratification by governments. It also undertakes special tasks assigned by the General Assembly or ECOSOC. It investigates allegations of violations of human rights and receives and processes communications related to such violations.

Under what is called the '1503 procedure', based on ECOSOC resolution 1503 adopted in 1970, the Commission deals in closed meetings with confidential communications about patterns of gross and systematic violations of human rights. Private complaints are discussed first in the Sub-Commission on Prevention of Discrimination and Protection of Minorities. If that body concludes that there seems to be 'a consistent pattern of gross and reliably attested violations of human rights', it refers the complaint to the Commission, which may then investigate further. The fact that such complaints are taken up may have a certain corrective effect, the more so because it is now common practice that the chairman of the Commission announces, after the meeting, the names of the states that were discussed under the 1503 procedure.

In its public meetings, the Commission may discuss human rights situations in all parts of the world. ECOSOC resolution 1235, adopted in 1967, allows both members and non-members of the Commission to raise violations of human rights anywhere. This may lead to resolutions with recommendations to be submitted to ECOSOC and to the General Assembly. It may also lead to further study of the problem, for example by a working group or special rapporteur. The latter possibility has been widely used by the Commission with the appointment of *country rapporteurs* on Bolivia, Chile, Guatemala and Romania in the past. There are now such rapporteurs on Afghanistan, Cuba, El Salvador, Equatorial Guinea, Haiti, Iran, Myanmar, the Occupied Arab Territories, Rwanda, Sudan and the former Yugoslavia.[4] In the wake of the Gulf War after Iraq's invasion of Kuwait, the Commission appointed two special rapporteurs for Iraq in 1991, one to study violations of human rights by Iraq and the second the violations committed in occupied Kuwait by Iraqi forces. Working groups study the human rights situation in South Africa and the Israeli Occupied Territories. Furthermore, it has appointed *thematic rapporteurs* on summary and arbitrary executions, on torture, on religious intolerance, on the use of mercenaries, the sale of children, violence against women, states of emergency, racism, racial discrimination, xenophobia and related intolerance, freedom of expression and independence of the judiciary. Working groups deal with the problem of enforced or involuntary disappearances and with arbitrary detention.[5] A special case among thematic mechanisms is the independent expert on property, appointed in 1991. Their reports are presented in the public meetings of the Commission, where governments can give their reactions to the reports.[6] That is also the case with the annual report of the *Sub-Commission on Prevention of Discrimination and Protection of Minorities.* The twenty-six members of the Sub-Commission are selected in their personal capacity, although it is well known that some maintain rather close relations with their governments. Not-withstanding its name, the Sub-Commission deals with studies on a broad range of human rights, which it submits to the Commission. The Sub-

Commission meets annually for four weeks in August during which it examines studies that it has commissioned to special rapporteurs. It plays an important role at an early stage of the 1503 procedure mentioned before.

Commission and Sub-Commission receive secretarial and administrative support from the UN Centre for Human Rights in Geneva, which suffers from understaffing and under-financing. A problem in both human rights bodies is the membership of governments (individual experts in the case of the Sub-Commission) that may themselves be guilty of gross human rights violations. Nevertheless, the human rights concerns of the two bodies are far-reaching. Their activities have put an end to the notion that human rights violations are solely a matter within the national sovereignty of states. Furthermore, it should be pointed out that their resolutions are often strongly politically motivated.[7]

The Commission may invite representatives of non-member states or liberation movements to take part in its deliberations on a non-voting basis. Specialized agencies and certain other intergovernmental organizations may also take part in discussions on topics of concern to them. Finally, a unique feature of the Commission on Human Rights is that along with the formal members of the body are seated a large number of non-governmental organizations with consultative status. They have the right to address the Commission, take part in its debates and to have written statements circulated as United Nations documents. Their presence gives support and provides added legitimacy to its activities.

Commission and Sub-Commission have few effective sanctions at their disposal to help put their findings into practice. In the final instance, the only weapon they possess is the weapon of publicity. That may be quite effective, as most governments dislike having their violations of human rights publicly discussed.

UN Human Rights Committee[8]

The International Covenant on Civil and Political Rights provides for a Human Rights Committee (to be distinguished from the *Commission* on Human Rights) that consists of eighteen persons 'of high moral character and recognized competence in the field of human rights'. Nominated by governments, they serve in a personal capacity, although again some of the members – being former or even present ambassadors – maintain close relations with their governments. The Committee usually meets three times a year. The states parties to the Covenant must submit periodic reports to the Committee on any national measures giving effect to the relevant rights and on the progress made in the enjoyment of those rights. The reporting governments are given the opportunity to expound their report in public sessions of the Committee and answer questions from Committee members. A major problem is that many States Parties are far behind in meeting their reporting obligations, while the Committee for its part lags behind in dealing with the reports.

A specific authorization obliges the Committee to deal with complaints by a state that another state has failed to fulfill its obligations. This procedure is limited to states that have recognized in advance this competence of the Committee. So far, only forty-four states have done so. Finally, if it adheres to an optional protocol, a state allows individuals subject to its jurisdiction to communicate to the Committee that they are victims of violations by that state of any rights set out in the Covenant. The Committee, after having determined that the communication is admissible under the protocol, must bring the complaint to the attention of the state concerned. That state must submit within six months a written explanation or statement clarifying the matter and the remedy taken. The Committee then considers the communication in light of all available information and forwards its views to the state and the individual concerned. Over the years, the Committee has built up an important body of case law, based on 300-odd cases, and it has formulated a number of general comments which constitute an important source of interpretation of many substantive articles of the Covenant. By the winter of 1996, 130 states had ratified or acceded to the Covenant; 84 states had ratified the first Optional Protocol.

Capital punishment, though not forbidden in the Covenant, is limited to the most serious crimes in accordance with the law in force at the time of the commission of the crime. It may not be imposed for crimes committed by persons below 18 years of age or carried out on pregnant women. In 1989, the General Assembly adopted an optional protocol against the death penalty. States that become parties to it are bound not to carry out executions. By the winter of 1996, only 28 states had acceded to this protocol.

Committee for Economic, Social and Cultural Rights

In 1985, the Economic and Social Council (ECOSOC) decided to establish a Committee for Economic, Social and Cultural Rights, consisting of eighteen individual experts. This committee considers national reports that states parties to the International Covenant on Economic, Social and Cultural Rights must submit periodically to ECOSOC on the measures they have adopted and the progress made in achieving the observance of the included rights. The Committee invites representatives of the reporting states to take part in its deliberations. It meets yearly for a period of at most three weeks and reports its findings to ECOSOC. ECOSOC may make recommendations of a general nature on these matters to the relevant organs of the United Nations. Under the provisions of this Covenant, individuals may not complain directly to an international body about violations of these rights. The Covenant serves as a standard of aspiration and means of judging progress towards a broad list of economic, social and cultural benefits. By the winter of 1996, it had been ratified by 131 states.

Committee on the Elimination of Racial Discrimination

The International Convention on the Elimination of All Forms of Racial Discrimination provides for the establishment of a committee of eighteen members, who are elected in their personal capacity by the states parties to the Convention for a term of four years. It meets twice a year and reports annually to the General Assembly. The Committee examines the information placed before it by states parties to the Convention. It is common practice that representatives of the reporting state attend the meeting of the Committee and answer questions from the Committee members. From time to time, it comments upon particular situations involving racial discrimination or draws them to the attention of the General Assembly. So far, only fourteen states have recognized the competence of the Committee to deal with communications from individuals within their jurisdiction and to prepare proposals and recommendations in regard to such communications.

Committee on the Elimination of Discrimination against Women

The Convention on the Elimination of All Forms of Discrimination against Women provides for the establishment of a committee of twenty-three members, who are elected in their personal capacity by the states parties to the Convention. The Committee meets annually for a period of two weeks. Its main task is to consider the reports that are periodically submitted by the states parties to the Convention on the legislative, judicial, administrative or other measures which they have adopted to give effect to the provisions of the Covenant and on the progress made in this respect. The Committee reports annually on its activities through ECOSOC to the General Assembly. Its report may contain suggestions and general recommendations based on the examination of reports and information received from the states parties.

Committee against Torture

The Convention against Torture and other Cruel, Inhuman or Degrading Treatment or Punishment provides for the establishment of a committee of ten experts which must consider the periodic reports submitted by the states parties on the measures they have taken to give effect to their undertaking under the Convention. If the Committee receives reliable information that torture is being systematically practised in the territory of a state party, it may designate one or more of its members to make a confidential inquiry. In agreement with that state, such an inquiry may include a visit to its territory. The Committee will transmit its findings to the state concerned together with any comments or suggestions which seem appropriate in view of the situation. All these activities are confidential. The Committee may, after consultation with the state concerned, decide to include a summary account of the results of the proceedings in its annual report. The lodging of complaints by states or by individuals with reference to non-compliance with the obligations of the Convention are only possible if the state concerned has explicitly recognized such a complaint procedure. So far, only twenty-nine states have done so.

Efforts are now under way to have the Commission on Human Rights adopt an optional protocol to the Convention against Torture providing for the regular inspection of places of detention throughout the world, similar to the provisions in the European Convention against Torture. This would greatly add to the power of the Committee against Torture in supervising implementation of the provisions of the Convention.

International Labour Organisation

The International Labour Organisation (ILO) has developed a mechanism of supervising the implementation of the conventions which it has adopted. A number of labour conventions, adopted by ILO, require periodical reporting by the states parties. Any employers' or workers' organisation may make a representation to the ILO that any of the members has failed to secure the effective observance of a convention to which it is a party. In addition, there exists the possibility of a complaints procedure in case of non-compliance. The general complaints procedure may be initiated by a member-state or by the Governing Body of ILO either on its own initiative or on receipt of a complaint by a delegate to the International Labour Conference. The Governing Body may decide to appoint a commission of inquiry, which will report to it and to the governments concerned.

Complaints regarding alleged violations of the freedom of association rights can be submitted by governments as well as employers' and workers' associations. Complaints against any member of the ILO that is alleged to have violated the fundamental principle of freedom of association can be filed irrespective of whether that member has ratified the freedom of association conventions. Such complaints can lead to rather negative publicity for the government in question, which in itself may be an effective sanction. Poland is a famous example, being accused in 1982 of violating the convention on freedom of association because of its suppression of the free trade-union *Solidarnósc*. For a while Poland refused to pay its regular financial assessment and did not participate in the work of ILO.[9]

UNESCO

The Convention against Discrimination in Education provides that the states parties will report on the legislative and administrative provisions which they have adopted and other action they have taken for the application of the Convention. These reports are submitted to the General Conference of UNESCO. According to an optional protocol, states parties may address communications to a conciliation and good offices commission, consisting of eleven members elected in their personal capacity, that another state is not giving effect to a provision of the Convention. The Commission will ascertain the facts and try to reach an amicable solution. If no solution is reached, its report can indicate the recommendation it has made for reaching a solution. The protocol contains no provision for dealing with complaints from individuals. John Humphrey has rightly remarked that, given the fact that states on the whole are re-luctant to bring other states before an international body, 'the implementation system created by the Protocol is not a strong one'.[10]

REGIONAL ARRANGEMENTS

In addition to the global systems established within the framework of the United Nations, there are regional arrangements of international supervision of human rights. Such regional arrangements have been established by the Council of Europe, the Organization of American States (OAS) and the Organization of African Unity (OAU).

European Convention on Human Rights

Most of the thirty-two member-states of the Council of Europe are parties to the Convention for the Protection of Human Rights and Fundamental Freedoms. That conven-tion contains a great number of standards of civil and politi-cal rights. It provides for the establishment of a European Commission of Human Rights and a European Court of Human Rights.[11]

In practice, each state party to the Convention nominates one member of the Commission. The members of the Commission are elected in their personal capacity by the Committee of Ministers for a term of six years. The Commission holds sixteen sessions of one or two weeks each year. The meetings of the Commission are held in private. The Commission may receive applications from any person, non-governmental organisation or group of individuals claiming to be the victim of a violation by a state party of any of the human rights provisions mentioned in the Convention. The Commission may only deal with the matter after all domestic remedies have been exhausted and within a period of six months from the date on which the final deci-sion at the domestic level was taken. The Commission func-tions to a great extent as a screen: the majority of petitions

are, for all kinds of reasons, declared inadmissible. In the
case of a petition that is admitted, the Commission tries first
to arrive at a friendly settlement. If a solution is not reached,
the Commission draws up a report on the facts and states its
opinion as to whether the facts found disclose a breach by
the state concerned of its obligations under the Convention.
The case may then be referred within three months to the
European Court of Human Rights which takes a final decision. If the question is not referred to the Court, the
Committee of Ministers will decide whether or not there has
been a violation of the Convention.

The Convention also provides for the possibility of an
inter-state complaint. Every state party to the Convention
has the right to lodge with the Commission a complaint of
any alleged breach of the Convention by any other state
party. This provision has not remained a dead-letter. In
1967, the Scandinavian states and the Netherlands submitted an interstate complaint against Greece, because of the
human rights situation under the military regime that governed the country at the time. Greece thereupon withdrew
from the Council of Europe, but the Commission on
Human Rights nevertheless submitted a report in which it
concluded that a number of human rights violations, including torture, had taken place. In 1982, the Scandinavian
states, France and the Netherlands submitted an inter-state
complaint against Turkey claiming that human rights under
the Convention were being violated by the Turkish military
regime. This complaint led to a friendly settlement in 1985
whereby Turkey committed itself to report periodically on
the measures it had taken with regard to its internal law and
practice so as to ensure the effective implementation of the
provisions of the Convention, especially with regard to conditions and procedures of detention.[12] Turkey did submit
three such reports. Since then, the inter-state complaint
procedure has not been used any more, although one
might argue that, for example in the case of Turkey, there
was still ample reason to do so.

The number of members of the European Court, who are
elected by the Parliamentary Assembly, is equal to the

number of members of the Council of Europe. In practice, each member of the Council appoints one member of the Court. It deals only with cases that are submitted by the Commission, by the state whose national is an alleged victim, by the state which referred the case to the Commission or the state against which the complaint has been lodged.

There is no right of appeal against decisions of the Court. The states undertake to abide by the decision of the Court in any case to which they are parties. The Court is not authorized, however, to quash decisions of national courts or to review national legislation. Decisions of the Commission and the Court may have important consequences. An example was the judgment of 1976 on interrogation techniques used by British military and police in Northern Ireland. The Commission considered this a matter of torture, while the Court decided that it amounted to inhuman treatment. Other important decisions dealt with the prohibition of corporal punishment, the prohibition of certain measures of secret surveillance such as wire-tapping, the stopping and delaying of correspondence, freedom of the press, fair trial, and respect for family life.

The supervision mechanisms of the European Convention are the most extensive and most effective existing procedures of implementation of international human rights standards. For a number of years already, the system has suffered from its own success. So many appeals are made to the European judicial organs that considerable delays occur in the handling of the cases. A considerable number of proposals was discussed to speed up the process. This led in 1994 to the adoption of Protocol No. 11, whose main feature is that a new single Court will replace the two existing supervisory organs, the Commission and the Court. When the Protocol has entered into force, individuals will have direct access to this new Court.[13]

Organization of American States

In 1948, the Charter of the Organization of American States (OAS) was adopted, together with the American Declaration of the Rights and Duties of Man as a set of standards in the field of human rights. In 1959, the Inter-American Commission on Human Rights was created. In 1969, the American Convention on Human Rights was adopted, creating the Inter-American Court of Human Rights, while the Commission continued to coexist. The provisions of the OAS Charter and the American Declaration of the Rights and Duties of Man, which apply to all members of the OAS, are supervised by the Inter-American Commission. The provisions of the Convention, which only apply to the states parties to the Convention, are supervised by the Inter-American Commission and the Inter-American Court.[14]

The Inter-American Commission on Human Rights has seven members elected by the General Assembly of the OAS to act in their individual capacity. Its aim is to promote the observance and defence of human rights in the continent as well as to serve as a consultative body for the OAS in this field. It may accept petitions from individuals, groups of individuals or non-governmental organizations. As in the case of the European Convention, national remedies must be exhausted before the Commission may deal with a petition. Furthermore, the Commission can conduct an investigation of its own and prepare a report on the human rights situation in a particular country. It may request information from the parties, conduct hearings or – with the approval of the government concerned – have a special committee visit the country under investigation. Thus, in the past, the Commission has issued reports on Bolivia, Chile, Cuba, El Salvador, Guatemala, Haiti, Panama, Paraguay, Peru and Suriname. During 1994, the Commission carried out visits to the Bahamas, Ecuador, Guatemala, Haiti and Jamaica. Its reports are usually submitted to the OAS General Assembly.

The reports of the Inter-American Commission may be far-reaching, as shown for example when in 1987 it found the United States guilty of violation of articles I and II of the American Declaration, in a case of application of the death penalty. It was the first time that an intergovernmental body had found the United States in violation of an international human rights norm.[15] The Convention provides also for the possibility of inter-state complaints, if both the complaining state and the state against which the complaint is lodged have explicitly recognized the competence of the Commission for this purpose. However, so far this procedure has never been put into practice.

The Inter-American Court consists of seven members elected by a majority vote of the states parties to the Convention. All seven judges participate in each Court decision. It meets in regular sessions twice a year in San José, Costa Rica. It decides on disputes brought before it by states parties to the Convention or by the Inter-American Commission relating to charges that a state party has violated the Convention. It may also render advisory opinions at the request of any member of the OAS or organs of the organization on the interpretation of the Convention and other human rights treaties, and on the conformity of national laws of the states with these treaties. For many years the Court had ruled on very few contentious cases, but more recently its workload has somewhat increased.[16] The Court has rendered several final decisions on cases brought forward by the Inter-American Commission. Sentences have been passed in three cases against Honduras, two cases against Suriname and one case each against Argentina, Colombia, Peru and Venezuela. The governments of Argentina and Venezuela have admitted the veracity of the facts of the case. Several other cases are still pending. Honduras has not yet paid the full compensation it was ordered to pay to the relatives of two 'disappeared' persons. Towards the winter of 1996, sixteen of the twenty-five states parties to the Convention had recognized the jurisdiction of the Court.

The Inter-American Commission is different from the European Commission in that it can itself take the initiative to deal with a case and a person need not be a victim himself to bring a case before the Commission. This gives it a stronger position in the protection of human rights. When conducting an investigation in a particular country, the Commission may accept all information that is supplied, irrespective of formal criteria of admissibility as evidence.

Such local visits provide the Commission with the opportunity to become acquainted with the details of gross human rights violations. The affected governments have not taken kindly to the active role of the Inter-American human rights organs. At recent meetings of the OAS General Assembly, the Inter-American Commission has been repeatedly criticized among other things for intervening in the internal affairs of member-states. Yet, other states have defended its independent position.[17]

In 1987, the Inter-American Convention to Prevent and Punish Torture came into force. By the winter of 1996, thirteen states had become party to this convention. A convention to prevent and punish forced disappearances of persons was adopted in 1994, as well as a convention on the prevention, punishment and eradication of violence against women; by the winter of 1996, the latter convention had been ratified by fifteen states. Talks have begun on the preparation of an inter-American instrument for the protection of indigenous peoples.

African Charter on Human Rights and Peoples' Rights

The African Charter on Human and Peoples' Rights (the 'Charter of Banjul') was adopted by the Organization of African Unity (OAU) in 1981 and came into force in 1986. The human rights listed are largely derived from earlier international human rights instruments such as the Universal Declaration and the two international covenants. A new and 'African' character is supplied by the list of 'peoples' rights' in the Charter. Among these are the right to self-determination, the right of peoples to freely dispose of their wealth and natural resources, the right to economic, social and cultural development, the right to peace and security and the right to a general satisfactory environment. The term 'people' is not defined, but coincides in practice with the population living on the territories of the states parties to the Charter. Another specific character of the Charter is the mentioning of duties that apply both to state parties and to individuals.

The Charter provides for an African Commission on Human and Peoples' Rights which started to function in 1987. The Commission consists of eleven members who are elected in their personal capacity for a term of six years by the Assembly of Heads of State and Government of the OAU. It was envisaged as a body to *promote* rather than to *protect* human rights.[18]

The Commission, which meets twice annually, deals with communications of a state party on violations of the Charter by another state party, if efforts to reach a friendly settlement have failed and after all local remedies have been exhausted. The Commission may also deal with communication from other, non-state sources. It reports to the Assembly of Heads of State and Government. Its reports are confidential, unless the Assembly decides otherwise. Independent observers consider the proceedings of the Commission as unnecessarily restrictive.[19]

Each state party must submit a periodic report on the legislative or other measures taken with a view to giving effect to the rights and freedoms recognized in the Charter. This obligation has gradually been put into practice, but comparatively few states have provided the necessary information. By 1992 only seven had submitted their reports, some of which (Nigeria!) contained insufficient information.[20] By the winter of 1996, all African states, except for Eritrea, Ethiopia, Swaziland and South Africa, had acceded to the Charter. While this is undoubtedly a positive development, on the whole the system has faced considerable difficulties. The African Commission has been confronted with a chronic lack of finances. Its secretariat is understaffed and the Commission lacks even the most elementary infrastructure such as office equipment and other administrative support.[21] The UN Centre of Human Rights and a number of non-governmental organizations as well as private foundations supply financial and organizational support. While such support is of course welcome, in the end the African states will have to supply the financial means of support themselves, if only to prevent the Commission from receiving too much of a foreign 'non-African' image.

The Charter does not provide for an African Court of Human Rights. This means that, unlike the European and Inter-American conventions, in the African case final decisions are left to the heads of state and government. This means also that the African system has, so far, been dominated more by political than by judicial considerations. The system is, however, still very much in development. Efforts are being made to learn from European and Inter-American experiences. Non-governmental organizations are emphasizing the need for an African human rights regime that is truly independent of governments. The future of the system will very much depend on the degree of success of such efforts.

CONCLUSION

The intergovernmental organizations dealt with in this chapter offer governments ample opportunity to express themselves on human rights matters. At the UN Commission on Human Rights they can do so by calling attention to violations of human rights in other states and by formulating conclusions and recommendations. If they are not themselves represented in such bodies, they can exert influence in the appointment of individual experts. Sometimes, governments nominate individuals who are directly related to them, even if these experts are supposed to be acting 'in a personal capacity'. This offers governments the opportunity of influencing matters.

The submission of inter-state complaints under the European Convention on Human Rights should of course fit in a government's foreign policy. The submission of a complaint against Turkey and its later friendly settlement was a case in point. Under the American Convention of Human Rights, governments may influence the activities of the Inter-American Commission by questioning the human rights situation in other countries. The situation under the African Charter is far from clear in this respect at present. Asia and the Pacific do not yet have a regional international organization, nor is there a regional arrangement in the area of human rights.

By way of summary one may conclude that intergovernmental organizations, in addition to their important work in the field of standard-setting, are increasing their activities with regard to the implementation of those standards.

Part II
Specific

7 The United States

AMERICAN FOREIGN POLICY: A COMBINATION OF MORALISM AND REALISM

From its very beginning the foreign policy of the United States has been typified by a combination of ethical principles and national interests. Americans often claim to know what is good for the world and want to set an example. In practice, this dual attitude has had conflicting consequences. At some points in time it has meant a policy of non-engagement, if not isolationism; at other moments, it has meant internationalism and an active engagement in world politics.

The principle of setting an example to other nations while at the same time avoiding political links with foreign countries was reflected in the famous farewell address of the first American president, George Washington. The avoidance of 'entangling alliances' was also favoured by his successor, Thomas Jefferson. The Monroe doctrine, formulated in 1823, explicitly limited the engagement of the United States to the American continent. A similar approach can be found in the neo-isolationism of the 1920s and 1930s in this century. On the other hand, there were also years of active engagement. The United States entered the First World War under Woodrow Wilson 'to make the world safe for democracy'. He argued for the maintenance of world order by means of international arbitration and jurisdiction. However, the League of Nations, which was in many ways the brainchild of this American President, was never approved by the US Senate and consequently the United States never became a member.

In 1941, President Franklin Delano Roosevelt, as a result of the war, formulated his famous four freedoms: freedom of speech and expression, freedom to worship God, freedom from want and freedom from fear.[1] Thus a number of important human rights became explicit goals of American foreign policy.

In this connection it should be emphasized that human rights has always been a major theme of American *domestic* policy. The Declaration of Independence of 1776 mentions life, liberty and the pursuit of happiness as inalienable rights of all men. The first ten amendments to the American Constitution, the 'Bill of Rights', encompass a number of basic human rights. The fight for the abolishment of slavery in the nineteenth century and the civil rights movement for equal rights for the black population and other minority groups in this century, point to human rights as a basic theme of American domestic policy.

American foreign policy has always been a mixture of idealism and realism. It gives evidence of a certain measure of moralism, of ethical principles, based on the idea that the United States will bring good to the world. At the same time, a careful eye is kept on preserving its own interests. Lloyd Jensen, an American political scientist, has written about the tendency in American foreign policy 'to develop legal and moralistic arguments to rationalize foreign policy choices'.[2] Americans tend to believe in their own rhetoric. They believe, in the words of a speech of a deputy assistant secretary of human rights and humanitarian affairs, that in the field of human rights they have 'something unique to offer to the world'.[3] In turn, they may become rather annoyed if others reason along similar lines and claim to pursue an even more moral foreign policy. Few foreign statesmen evoked at the time as much irritation in the United States as the Indian leader Pandit Nehru, a strong advocate of non-engagement and 'positive neutralism' (positive in the sense that he did not want to align his country with either of the two major power blocs, but nevertheless wanted to contribute to finding a solution to the Cold War). An irritated US Secretary of State, John Foster Dulles, reacted by proclaiming: 'You can't be neutral between right and wrong.'

In brief, American foreign policy is characterized by thinking in terms of good and evil, of moralism, personified in statesmen such as Woodrow Wilson, John Foster Dulles and Jimmy Carter. At the same time there is a strong touch of realism, based on reasons of state, personified in former diplomat George Kennan[4] and former Secretary of State Henry Kissinger. The latter explicitly rejected the incorporation of human rights among the aims of foreign policy:

> I believe it is dangerous for us to make the domestic policy of countries around the world a direct objective of American foreign policy.... The protection of basic human rights is a very sensitive aspect of the domestic jurisdiction of ... governments.[5]

HUMAN RIGHTS POLICY

Both lines of thinking – moralism and self-interest – are found alternately or simultaneously in American foreign policy.[6] The human rights policy of the United States should be seen in this framework. Putting an emphasis on human rights has on the one hand a strong moralistic character, as in the case of President Jimmy Carter.[7] On the other hand, it also has a strong instrumental character: by emphasizing human rights, other more general foreign policy objectives may be attained, as seems to have been the case with the Reagan and Bush administrations.[8]

The ideal situation from the point of view of policy-makers arises if considerations of power politics and moral ethical considerations coincide. For many years this was the case with American foreign policy *vis-à-vis* the Soviet Union.[9] In that case, the United States could express its concern over human rights without having to fear that this might be detrimental to its security interests. That enabled Jeane Kirkpatrick, who during the Reagan administration served for a while as ambassador to the United Nations, to make an often cited distinction between *authoritarian* regimes where there is hope for improvement (in the sense of democratization) and *totalitarian* regimes, meaning the communist countries, where such improvement is extremely unlikely.[10] She criticized the Carter administration because it had made the mistake of withholding support from American allies who had been guilty of violations of human rights. Later developments in Eastern Europe have clearly proved her wrong. Cyrus Vance, who served as Secretary of State under Carter, was one among many commentators who took issue with Kirkpatrick on grounds of principle: 'Kirkpatrick's thesis damaged America's image as a beacon of freedom and a wise and humane champion of human rights.'[11]

Presidents Nixon and Ford paid relatively little attention to human rights in their foreign policy.[12] It was President Jimmy Carter (1976–80) who particularly made human rights a major item of American foreign policy.[13]

LEGISLATION

A committee of the House of Representatives, headed by Congressman Donald Fraser, had already at the time of the presidency of Richard Nixon held hearings about human rights. These resulted in Section 116 of the Foreign Assistance Act. The pertinent subparagraph (a) of that section determines that the government of the United States may give no assistance to the government of any country which engages in a consistent pattern of gross violations of internationally recognized human rights. These include torture or cruel, inhuman, or degrading treatment or punishment, prolonged detention without charges, or other flagrant denials of the right to life, liberty and the security of person, 'unless such assistance will directly benefit the needy people in such country'.[14] If such a government is nevertheless given assistance, the President must report to Congress on the special circumstances which make this necessary.[15]

In 1976, Congress amended section 502b of the International Security Assistance and Arms Export Control Act. This amendment entailed a prohibition of security assistance and arms sales to countries which are guilty of the systematic and gross violation of internationally recognized human rights. Only under 'extraordinary circumstances' or to protect vital national interests may the President deviate from this rule. This escape clause has led to considerable debate, because human rights organizations have felt that the United States government has used it too often to give military support to friendly governments such as those of President Marcos of the Philippines and President Suharto of Indonesia, both of whom have been responsible for gross human rights violations. Under President Carter, military support to a number of Latin American governments was terminated because of their human rights policies. His successors, Reagan and Bush, did not terminate any military assistance programmes for this reason. In 1990, Congress inserted section 582 into the annual appropriations bill under the Foreign Assistance Act, requiring the State Department to submit to Congress a listing of countries whose governments are found to engage in consistent patterns of gross violations of internationally recognized human rights. In addition, the State Department must report how the aid granted to such countries is being used to promote human rights and how the United States has avoided being identified with human rights violations in those countries.

Finally, there is legislation relating to the activities of the World Bank and its affiliated institutions with regard to loans to countries where human rights violations are taking place. According to section 701 of the International Financial Institutions Act of 1977, American Executive Directors of international financial institutions should oppose all financial or technical assistance to such countries, unless such assistance is directed specifically to programmes serving the basic human needs of the citizens.[16]

Furthermore, Congress has adopted legislation that requires the Department of State to submit an annual public report on the human rights situation in countries receiving American foreign aid, including information on the number of political prisoners, torture, arbitrary arrests and detention, arbitrary restriction of existing political rights,

extralegal executions and unfair trials. Later, this reporting
obligation was extended to cover all states members of the
United Nations. All American embassies must collect
information about the human rights situation in their
country of accreditation. The reporting covers only civil
and political rights; economic, social and cultural rights are
excluded. The latter are not considered to be human rights,
but mainly regarded as ambitions or aspirations.[17] The
quality of the reports has steadily improved over the years.[18]
Moreover, it is of major importance that this type of public
reporting takes place, as it offers the opportunity to
members of Congress and others to discuss the human
rights situation in various countries on the basis of an
official document supplied by the US government. The
report over 1994 covered 193 countries.

In spite of the extensive legislation on the subject, a considerable amount of criticism has been levelled at the implementation process. The executive branch and Congress
have been criticized for routinely granting security assistance to governments guilty of gross human rights violations,
yet considered strategically vital in stopping the spread of
communism. The Lawyers Committee for Human Rights
has called for a comprehensive review of US security assistance policies and practices in light of current security and
strategic needs.[19]

HELSINKI PROCESS

After the signing of the Helsinki Final Act on security and
cooperation in Europe in 1975, a commission for security
and cooperation in Europe was created to monitor and en-
courage progress in implementing the provisions of the
Helsinki human rights accords. It is made up of nine
Senators, nine Representatives and one official each from
the Departments of State, Commerce and Defense. The fact
that members of Congress as well as members of the administration serve on the Commission makes it unique in its
kind. It organizes hearings and commissions studies on the

situation with regard to human rights, with a special focus on the countries of Central and Eastern Europe. These studies sometimes lead to concrete recommendations for government policy.

RECENT US PRESIDENTS

President Carter devoted a large part of his speeches to human rights, which he considered a major item of foreign policy. He felt that the commitment of the United States to human rights should be of an absolute nature: 'Our moral sense dictates a clearcut preference for those societies which share with us an abiding respect for individual human rights.'[20] He was well aware of the fact that his policy pronouncements were to a large degree verbal announcements: 'But I also believe that it is a mistake to undervalue the power of words and of the ideas that words embody. In the life of the human spirit, words *are* action.'[21]

Presidents Reagan and Bush emphasized in their human rights policy mainly activities outside the public limelight.[22] Such a policy is by definition unverifiable and difficult to demonstrate. In the words of deputy secretary Elliott Abrams, 'Traditional diplomacy has the drawback of being least visible precisely where it is most successful.'[23] However, under Reagan, increasing public attention was paid to the human rights situation in countries as diverse as Cuba and South Africa, as well as the Soviet Union, the 'evil empire'. The Bush administration began to pay more attention than before to human rights violations by America's longtime ally in the Middle East, Israel, while the collapse of communism in Eastern Europe was partly acclaimed as a victory for United States human rights policy. Both administrations found it difficult to formulate a consistent policy *vis-à-vis* China. While on the one hand critical of China's violation of a number of fundamental human rights, the United States has made an effort to maintain a smooth working relationship with that government. The Clinton administration has been strongly criticized by human rights activists for renewing in May 1993 China's most-favoured-nation status in its trade relations with the United States for at least one year. In spite of continued negative reports about the human rights situation in China, President Clinton, urged by US business interests, decided in the spring of 1994 to renew the most-favoured nation status of China.

CIVIL SERVICE

In 1974, two years before the election of Jimmy Carter, there was only one official in the State Department who dealt with human rights on a full-time basis. He was responsible for preparing US government positions on human rights issues at the United Nations.[24] In the course of 1974 and 1975, as the result of pressure exercised by the Fraser Committee, more officials were appointed in the State Department to deal with human rights, but their role remained limited, because Secretary of State Henry Kissinger was himself not very much interested in the subject. At one point he even forbade the release of a report prepared by the State Department on human rights conditions in aid-recipient countries because he felt that neither the US security interest nor the human rights cause would be served by singling out individual states for public obloquy.[25]

Under President Carter, the apparatus dealing with human rights matters was substantially enlarged.[26] In the State Department a bureau was created headed by an assistant secretary of state for human and humanitarian affairs (Patricia Derian). The staff was enlarged to thirty persons, ten of whom dealt solely with human rights matters, while the others covered related issues such as refugees, disappearances and prisoners of war. An interdepartmental committee, chaired by Warren Christopher, who was later to become Secretary of State under President Clinton, dealt with the coordination of human rights policy with other policies, especially economic.[27] However, it has been pointed out that Carter and Derian did not succeed in interjecting human rights systematically into American foreign policy.[28]

Under Reagan and Bush the organization as designed by Carter was basically maintained.[29] The Senate rejected President Reagan's first candidate for the function of assistant secretary of state, among other reasons because he saw human rights policy entirely in terms of the battle against communism. The person who was eventually appointed, Elliott Abrams, was not known for his expertise in the field of human rights, but that may well have been the reason why he was considerably more successful than his predecessor in integrating human rights in American foreign policy.[30] The interdepartmental coordination committee has gradually lost most of its importance.[31]

RATIFICATION OF HUMAN RIGHTS TREATIES

In 1978, President Carter signed the two international human rights covenants and submitted them for approval to the Senate. That body was not very eager to approve the treaties, for a number of political and judicial reasons. There was considerable reluctance to accept the notion that American citizens should behave according to standards that were devised by the international community and supervised by an international body. Furthermore, many people feared that it would increase the power of the Federal Government at the expense of states' rights.[32]

It took until 1992 for the Senate finally to approve one of the two treaties, the International Covenant on Civil and Political Rights. It did not, however, accept the First Optional Protocol, which offers the possibility of individual complaints. Moreover, the United States declared that it did not regard the treaty as self-executing. This means that the treaty cannot be invoked in procedures before American courts. Finally, the United States has added a number of reservations, understandings and declarations to the treaty,[33] meaning that it has not accepted any commitments which go beyond what was already accepted under the provisions of the United States

Constitution. Thus it has, for example, rejected the provision of the treaty which rules out the application of the death penalty to persons who at the time the crime was committed were younger than eighteen. Also the notion of 'cruel, inhuman and degrading treatment or punishment' is restricted to the way in which it has been interpreted under the United States Constitution. These reservations and interpretations have not been accepted by a number of other States parties to the treaty. The Vienna Convention on the Law of Treaties provides states parties to a convention with the option of not accepting reservations made by another state party. Under somewhat similar circumstances a number of states parties to the genocide convention, including the United Kingdom, Sweden and the Netherlands, have rejected reservations made by the United States.[34]

Similar reluctance to enter into international commitments in the field of human rights has been the reason why the United States has not yet ratified many other international human rights treaties. However, in 1994, the United States became a party to the International Convention against Racial Discrimination and the Convention against Torture and other Cruel, Inhuman or Degrading Treatment or Punishment.[35]

FOREIGN AID

Two American political scientists, David Carleton and Michael Stohl, have tried to answer the question whether the human rights situation in aid-receiving countries makes any difference to the amount of American military aid. Their research produced the unanticipated conclusion that the most important factor in predicting the amount of money spent on aid was the assistance given in the previous year. There was hardly any difference in military aid given by the Carter and Reagan administrations.[36] They did find a large difference in rhetoric, and described Carter as 'long on rhetoric and short on action'.[37]

NON-GOVERNMENTAL ORGANIZATIONS

Non-governmental organizations have strongly criticized
United States foreign policy on human rights. Thus in 1987,
'Human Rights Watch' and the 'Lawyers Committee for
Human Rights' accused the Reagan administration of only
paying attention to human rights violations by its oppo-
nents, leaving out those by its allies. They cited American
condemnation of countries such as the Soviet Union,
Czechoslovakia, Cuba and Nicaragua and her silence on
human rights violations in Turkey, Indonesia, Kenya, South
Africa and Honduras. This kind of charge may have caused
the spectacular critical observations in the 1988 State
Department country report on the performance of the
Israeli army in the Occupied Territories.[38] In 1992, the
Lawyers Committee has reiterated its strongly voiced
criticism of US foreign policy.[39]

Some years before, deputy secretary Elliott Abrams,
whom we mentioned earlier, had declared in an interview
with a Dutch newspaper that the United States as a world
power had a different attitude from that of the West
European states toward the human rights situation in countries such as South Korea or Haiti: 'European human rights
policy is based on talk. And I can well imagine that if I were
Dutch, Swedish or Danish, this would be my policy, too.'[40]
He implied that the United States as a world power had to
be more careful than smaller nations in making pronouncements on human rights situations elsewhere, in view of the
greater consequences of such pronouncements. That may
be so. But one might add that those very consequences
make the policy choices of the American government in
this area therefore the more important.

AN EFFECTIVE HUMAN RIGHTS POLICY

The Reagan and Bush administrations have always strongly
emphasized the importance of adopting a human rights

policy that is truly effective. Michael Stohl and three other
political scientists have compared the results of the first two
years of the Carter and Reagan administrations, using material of Amnesty International. Among the 59 countries that
were studied, the human rights situation improved in five
during the Carter administration and in seven during
Reagan. The situation deteriorated in four countries during
the Carter period and in eight during Reagan. They conclude that the results of human rights policy under
President Reagan were not significantly better or worse than
under Carter. They do allocate some measure of importance to the moral support which the *victims* of human rights
violations received from public expressions of support by
President Carter. Reagan expressed himself less strongly on
the subject.[41]

CONCLUSION

American human rights policy fits clearly in the traditions
of American foreign policy. The objective of human rights
policy is either to create a better world or to contribute to
the interests in the field of national security and the
economy of the United States. Sometimes, both objectives
are at stake, if they are not in conflict with each other.

Human rights policy, as formulated by the President and
the Secretary of State, is, as always under the American constitutional system, strongly influenced by Congress. That
influence may be negative or positive. A negative influence
was exerted when the Senate refused to approve the most
important international human rights covenants, and finally
only approved the International Covenant on Civil and
Political Rights with strong reservations. While President
Carter had at least developed some activities in this field,
there were fewer on the part of Reagan and Bush. Positive
influence was exerted when legislation was adopted which
led to a separate section in the State Department dealing
with human rights, the annual country reports and the activities of Congress with regard to foreign economic aid,

military aid and American performance in the World Bank and other international financial institutions.

With regard to the implementation of the adopted legislation, there was a considerable difference in enthusiasm on the part of the team of President Carter and those of his successors, Reagan and Bush. A major difference was the way in which Carter expressed himself on human rights and the way in which he inspired others.[42] Though there may have been a difference of motivation, as far as concrete human rights policy is concerned, there appears to have been less difference between the Democratic and the two Republican administrations than one might have expected.

8 The Soviet Union and Its Successors

For the greater part of the post-Second World War period, international relations were dominated by the East–West conflict, the struggle between the two superpowers, the United States and the Soviet Union. In that struggle, human rights have played a role of considerable importance, especially since the signing of the Helsinki agreements of 1975 until the demise of the Soviet Union in 1991. Indeed, if one wants to understand world politics for the greater part of the twentieth century, the study of the foreign policy of the Soviet Union – as well as that of the United States – is indispensable. Although most of this is now a matter of the past, it is a still very recent past. Much of what is happening in Central and Eastern Europe can only be understood if one is aware of the major changes that have taken place very recently in political life in general in that part of the world, including in the area of human rights. That is why this book about the role of human rights in foreign policy contains a chapter on the foreign policy of what used to be the Soviet Union and its successors.

GENERAL FOREIGN POLICY

Albeit indispensable for the understanding of world politics, this does not mean that the foreign policy of the Soviet Union has always been easily understood. Winston Churchill in an often cited passage in his memoirs, once characterized Soviet foreign policy as a 'riddle wrapped in a mystery inside an enigma'.[1] Much has been said and written about the foundations of Soviet foreign policy.[2] Even with the benefit of hindsight, it is by no means easy to give a definitive judgement about the general ideas behind Soviet foreign policy. Concepts that were world-famous during the brief reign of Mikhail Gorbachev (1986–90) such as *perestroika* (economic reform), *glasnost* (freedom of the press) and *novoe myshlenie* (new foreign policy) have come and gone. What before used to be quite certain, became very much a matter of discussion under Gorbachev.

Was Soviet foreign policy mainly determined by ideological considerations? Or was it more a matter of 'czarism in overalls'?[3] That question used to be hotly debated by Sovietologists. The major feature that used to distinguish public policy of the Soviet Union and its allies from that of other states was the existence of a generally accepted, official doctrine: Marxism-Leninism. Much has been written about the question of whether the foreign policy of the Soviet Union was mainly determined by ideology or by more traditional Russian national interests of a military-strategic and economic nature. Among such interests are ice-free ports, security of the territorial borders by the creation of vassal states, the possession of its own sources of energy, etc.

The need for (more) territorial security has always been an important feature of Soviet foreign policy – the term 'encirclement complex' has been used in this regard. This need for security has been prompted by repeated past experiences with foreign aggression. The most important of these have been the Napoleonic invasion in the nineteenth century, those by the Germans in the First and Second World Wars, and western intervention during and after the 1917 revolution. Soviet expert Vernon Aspaturian has spoken in this regard of a 'dual quest for physical and psychological security'.[4]

The foreign as well as the domestic policy of the Soviet Union under Josef Stalin (its political leader between 1924 and 1953) was formulated in ideological terms. Foreign policy was directed toward the maintenance and strengthening of what was called international proletarian solidarity. Because in the Soviet Union, in contrast to most other countries, the proletarian revolution had already taken place, the international proletariat was expected to turn its loyalty toward the Soviet Union as the fatherland of socialism. That approach is well reflected in the following words by W.M. Chvostov, at the time chairman of the Soviet Academy for Pedagogical Sciences in Moscow:

> The foreign policy of the Soviet Union serves the interests of the classes and groups of socialist society – the working-class, the peasants, and the intelligentsia, in other words the interests of all the people and it thus depends on the people. That gives Soviet policy its great strength. The support of the people helps to guarantee the effective impact of Soviet policy on the outside world.
>
> As the origin and development of the Soviet Union have such a great and revolutionary impact on the present world and on the entire course of contemporary history, the maintenance and therefore the security of the Soviet Union is the most important factor in developing humanity toward socialism.[5]

Marxism-Leninism did not produce only one type of foreign policy. Friendly relations with the other socialist states were pursued, which were assumed to be dominated by the same atmosphere of harmony that was expected within communist societies after the withering-away of the state. But it might turn out to be necessary, in the interests of the security of the fatherland of socialism, to conclude alliances even with the enemies of socialism. These could even be its worst enemies, as was shown by the Nazi – Soviet non-aggression pact of 1939. Under the reign of party secretary Nikita Khrushchev (1953–64) the notion of 'peaceful coexistence' was developed.[6] That meant an important change of policy, as it explicitly recognized the possibility of peaceful development and 'peaceful competition' among different political and social-economic systems in the world.

For many years the dissemination of socialism coincided with the promotion of the interests of the Soviet Union abroad. By improving the position of the first and most powerful socialist state in the world, the position of socialism itself was considered to be strengthened. The Soviet Union could therefore for many years count on the loyal support of the communist parties in other countries. These assumed that the best and fastest way of promoting social-ism in their countries was to give support to the great social-ist brotherland. They could refer to developments in Poland, Romania, Hungary, Bulgaria, Czechoslovakia and the German Democratic Republic where – as a first step toward socialism – so-called 'people's democracies' were created in the aftermath of the Second World War. Small wonder that in Western Europe and North America com-munists were often accused of dual loyalty, if not outright treason.

HUMAN RIGHTS POLICY

Ideologically, there has always existed a major gap between the views of the socialist countries and the western coun-tries with respect to human rights. The West has always at-tached great value to the rights of the individual citizen *vis-à-vis* his own government. In the view of Marxism-Leninism the rights of the individual refer to his partici-pation in society rather than protection from society. The individual derives his rights from society.[7] When the General Assembly of the United Nations debated the Universal Declaration of Human Rights, Soviet delegate Andrei Vishinskij made an explicit reservation regarding the rights of individual persons in relation to his own state. Such ideas were not relevant for the USSR, where there were no rival classes. In such a society there could not be any antagonism between the government and the individ-ual, since the government was in fact the collective individ-ual. History had solved this problem in his country. The state and the individual were in harmony with each other; their interests coincided.[8] That was one of the reasons why the Soviet Union and its allies abstained when the vote was taken on the Universal Declaration.

According to Marxism-Leninism, human rights are pro-moted by the struggle of the oppressed and exploited masses against capitalism. In this sense, human rights are always class rights. The extent and content of human rights and freedoms and their implementation are conditioned in every state by the prevailing socio-economic system and the class structure of society.[9] Therefore there cannot be – contrary to what is commonly thought in the West – permanent and inalienable human rights that are valid for all human beings, at all times and in all situations.

While in the West civil and political rights receive most attention, Marxism-Leninism used to emphasize economic and social rights, preeminently the right to work, but also the right to health care and care of the elderly. Social-economic rights were seen as the foundation for the realisation of rights and liberties in other fields. In that sense, civil and political rights on the one hand, and economic, social and cultural rights on the other, are indeed indivisible.[10] The right to property, which is mentioned in the Universal Declaration, is in the socialist conception not considered to be a human right. The private ownership of the means of production is after all viewed as the major reason for the violation of human rights.

The emphasis on the importance of social and economic rights leads logically to an emphasis on the right to peace: people should be prevented from losing their means of subsistence through wars or other means of destruction. Human beings have the right to a peaceful life, without exploitation, without imperialistic, economic, nationalist or racist oppression, without the threat of ever new destructive weapons.[11]

Closely linked to the right to peace is the principle of non-intervention in the affairs of other nations. Such intervention would after all constitute a threat to the peace. Respect for internationally recognized human rights should, in the Soviet view, be left to the sovereign states.[12] The importance of the maintenance of national sovereignty was strongly emphasized by Soviet delegate Andrei Vishinskij during the debate in the UN General Assembly on the Universal Declaration of Human Rights. The independence and well-being of a nation depended on the principle of national sovereignty which was the sole protector of the smaller countries against the expansionist dreams of more powerful states.[13] In the Soviet view, cooperation among states in the field of human rights must go together with respect for the sovereign equality of all states and non-intervention in matters that belong essentially to their domestic jurisdiction. That doesn't alter the fact that there may be circumstances when states may become involved in the activities of other states. That situation occurs in the case of aggression, fascism, national-socialism, colonialism, apartheid, racism and mass unemployment. These are such serious and systematic violations of human rights that they can constitute a threat to world peace. In those cases, in the Soviet view, intervention by other states is permissible. In general, the principle of non-intervention takes precedence, unless it can be demonstrated that a violation of human rights constitutes a threat to international peace and security. The political practice of the Soviet Union has often been in violation of this principle, as the examples of Hungary 1956, Czechoslovakia 1968 and Afghanistan 1979 amply illustrate.

In Chapter 4 we discussed various interpretations of the prohibition of outside intervention as contained in the Helsinki Final Act (pp. 43–5). Bloed and Van Dijk have made the point that in the Russian language there is only one term used for the concepts of 'intervention' and 'interference'.[14] The mechanism first adopted in the CSCE Vienna Follow-up meeting (see Chapter 4, pp. 44–5) allows for a kind of foreign 'intervention' which in the past would have been unacceptable to the Soviet Union. The political changes connected with the coming to power of Mikhail Gorbachev and the acceptance by the West of holding a human rights conference in Moscow (which actually took place in 1991) may help to explain this change of attitude.

CHANGES IN HUMAN RIGHTS POLICY

For many years the Soviet Union – and the other Eastern European states in its wake – expressed views about human rights that differed strongly from those held by western states. Its emphasis on social and economic rights at the expense of civil and political rights and its emphasis on the principle of non-intervention and national sovereignty have already been mentioned. Also with regard to freedom of expression the government of the Soviet Union entertained different views. It was of the opinion that this freedom should not give fascists the right to freely express themselves:

> The USSR delegation had clearly stated that the only limitation to freedom that it required was the limitation of fascist propaganda and fascist activities ... [T]o argue that the prevention of fascist propaganda was impossible from the point of view of the principles of complete freedom was tantamount to applying the same attitude to laws which restrained the activities of various types of criminals, murderers, thieves, rogues etc.[15]

That was the third reason – next to the two already mentioned – why the Soviet Union, together with Byelorussia, Czechoslovakia, Poland, Ukraine, Yugoslavia, Saudi Arabia and South Africa, abstained in the vote on the Universal Declaration of Human Rights. That decision has more recently been marked by Soviet sources as a 'mistake'.[16] Forty years after its adoption by the General Assembly, Deputy Minister for Foreign Affairs, A.L. Adamishin, called the Universal Declaration an example of, and hope for, international cooperation: 'a universal guide through the turbulent sea of political passions surrounding human rights towards the shores of a new, more human civilization'.[17]

The political changes introduced by Mikhail Gorbachev have also had important repercussions for human rights. In foreign policy, for instance, there was a far more cooperative attitude from the Soviet Union at the negotiations in the framework of CSCE, and a more positive attitude toward the United Nations.[18] On the domestic front, scores of political prisoners were released in the reform of penal law, and there was a far more liberal attitude on the part of the authorities toward religious freedom and a remarkable improvement in the freedom of the press. As the Soviet authorities had previously always denied that there were any political prisoners in the Soviet Union, it came as no surprise when it was announced that the releases were of persons 'who in the West are called political prisoners'. The changed attitude of the Soviet authorities also manifested itself in its emigration policy. The number of Jewish persons who were allowed to leave the Soviet Union rose strongly. The semi-official 'Anti-Zionist Committee of the Soviet Public' was disbanded and replaced by an advisory committee for international cooperation in humanitarian and human rights matters.

The human rights organization Amnesty International, which in the past had often been very critical of the Soviet Union's internal human rights policies, released a report in 1989[19] in which it said that the Soviet perspective on human rights had shifted dramatically. Soviet authorities had made a public commitment to international human rights standards and supported new measures which allowed countries to monitor each other's human rights performance. New principles of criminal law had been published which would restrict the use of the death penalty and official proposals were made to give precedence to international standards over domestic law. Part of Amnesty's findings were based on the results of an unprecedented visit by Amnesty representatives at the invitation of the USSR Academy of Sciences in early 1989. This was remarkable because in the past Soviet authorities and the Soviet press used to attack Amnesty fiercely for its anti-Soviet partisanship and alleged links with British and American intelligence organizations.[20] Another human rights organization which received permission to visit the Soviet Union was the International Helsinki Federation for Human Rights, which in the past had been described as an enemy of the Soviet people.[21]

CONCLUSION

Soviet human rights policy before Gorbachev used to be rather simple to characterize. In its foreign policy: strong emphasis on non-intervention and national sovereignty, rejection of foreign involvement with what were seen as internal matters, further emphasis on economic and social rights. Domestically: rejection of the principle of rights of the individual *vis-à-vis* the state, repression of dissident political views, restriction of freedom of expression.

During the regime of Gorbachev major changes occurred, which have continued after the demise of the Soviet Union and its replacement by the Russian Federation and the other independent republics. One can now more or less safely conclude that the changes which were introduced under Gorbachev have on the whole been accepted and continued by his successors. In 1991 the Russian parliament established a constitutional court to review the constitutionality of international treaties, national laws and also the activities of high officials including the President. It is still a matter of debate whether the Court can test to what extent national rules are in accordance with international obligations. The new Russian Constitution refers rather vaguely to 'generally recognized international standards relating to human rights'. The value of the newly established legal institutions for daily practical life in Russia still remains to be demonstrated however.[22] An official report to President Yeltsin on Russia's human rights record in 1995 revealed widespread and systematic violations of the country's constitution. The report's author, Sergei Kovalyov, chairman of the presidential human rights committee, said that abuses were systematic and flagrant in many areas.

The major problems in the field of human rights in most of the successor states of the Soviet Union relate to the treatment of ethnic and linguistic minorities. The newly independent states tend to emphasize their homogeneity which often leads to the suppression of minorities. For instance, in the Baltic countries, the Russian speaking minorities have so far not been granted full citizenship. According to the 1989 census, the Russian Federation contains more than 130 different nationalities. The OSCE High Commissioner on National Minorities, Max van der Stoel, has visited Estonia in an effort to help to solve the problems

of the Russian minority. Some of the problems the Russian
Federation has to deal with are the following:

- the restoration of rights of peoples and ethnic
  groups which have been subjected to repression by
  Stalin (Crimean Tartars, Soviet Germans, Chechens,
  Cossacs);
- territorial and historical ambitions (Kabardians and
  Balkarians, North Osetia and Igushetia, Kalmykia
  and Astrachan);
- the centrifugal tendency of detachment of national
  republics and regions (Chechenia, Tartarstan,
  Jakutia);
- the social and economic decline in the regions with
  small indigenous peoples and ethnic groups (Border
  North and Far East);
- the influx of ethnic refugees from regions with
  armed ethnopolitical conflicts and wars;
- the precarious situation of ethnic Russians and
  Russian-speaking groups in national republics within
  the Russian Federation and in the newly independent nation-states, where Russians have become ethnic
  minorities.[23]

The position of the latter is very much a matter of
concern to the government of the Russian Federation. The
Russian delegate to the World Conference on Human
Rights in Vienna was clearly referring to the situation in the
Baltic countries when he stated: 'A democracy cannot be
recognized as genuine if it is only established for the "indigenous" population, while members of national minorities are either forced out of the country or made
outcasts.'[24] His speech differed rather considerably from
what his Soviet predecessor would have said, when he declared: '[W]e cannot accept references to the non-interference principle with regard to other countries ... when
violation of individual rights and freedoms is involved.'[25]
Time will tell whether the former Soviet republics will be
able to solve the present problems of a multi-ethnic and

pluralist society while maintaining fundamental international human rights standards. It will take a major effort to deal with these problems in a peaceful and civilized manner, in order to avoid a Yugoslavia-type quagmire.

The violent way in which the Government of the Russian Federation has been trying to bring the situation in Chechnia under control, is not a very promising sign.[26]

9 Western Europe

EUROPEAN UNION

The original treaties which form the basis of the European Community (nowadays the European Union) did not contain specific references to human rights. In the beginning, human rights did not constitute a major field of activities of the European Community.[1] In later years this has changed, however. The first important step was the adoption in 1977 of a Joint Declaration on the Protection of Fundamental Freedoms by the European Commission, the Council of Ministers and the European Parliament. In it the three institutions stressed 'the prime importance they attach to the protection of fundamental rights, as derived in particular from the constitutions of the Member States and the European Convention for the Protection of Human Rights and Fundamental Freedoms.'[2]

Originally, the European Parliament and the governments meeting in the framework of European Political Cooperation (EPC) were the bodies that paid most attention to human rights. The Treaty on European Union ('Maastricht Treaty'), which entered into force in November 1993, provides for a Common Foreign and Security Policy. Its objectives include explicitly 'to develop and consolidate democracy and the rule of law, and respect for human rights and fundamental freedoms.'[3] However, at the time of writing (early 1996) most of this Common Foreign and Security Policy is still very much in a preparatory stage. For the time being, foreign policy-making remains more a matter of intergovernmental cooperation than of Union-policy. Nevertheless, the main organs of the European Union are increasingly paying attention to the field of human rights.

Specific

THE EUROPEAN COMMISSION

Several members of the European Commission get involved on a more or less regular basis with human rights. The President of the Commission is charged with the coordination of such activities by the commissioners who deal with external political relations, external economic relations, North–South relations, humanitarian aid and immigration and asylum matters, respectively. Human rights matters in non-EU countries are dealt with by the commissioner who is responsible for that country, whereas the commissioner responsible for the Common Foreign and Security Policy is in charge of the coordination of the Commission's general policy on human rights and external relations. Human rights matters within EU member-states remain as a rule outside the authority of the Commission, but this may change with the upcoming revision of the Treaty on European Union (Maastricht Treaty) now that a large majority of Member States advocates accession of the European Union as a whole to the European Convention on Human Rights.

The question of accession has now been under discussion for a number of years. Such accession was recommended by the Commission as early as 1979, while it asked the Council of Ministers for a formal mandate in 1990, so that the actions of the EC institutions would be subject to control by the supervision mechanisms of the Convention. This proposal has also received the support of the European Parliament.[4] So far, this accession has not materialized, because of legal as well as political objections of the British and one or two other member-governments. The European Court of Justice in Luxembourg does, however, refer in its decisions to articles of the European Convention on Human Rights.[5]

Since 1984, a member of the General Secretariat has been charged with the coordination of the EU's human rights policy. This official refers documentation and information to the specific directorate-general that is responsible for the preparation of actual policy decisions. In 1988, a new directorate within the General Secretariat was charged with servicing intergovernmental cooperation among the member-states; this directorate had a member who specialized in human rights. This directorate assists the President of the Commission in his coordinating activities. In 1993, it became part of a new directorate for external political relations, and thereby lost its coordinating role which it had been entrusted with when part of the General Secretariat.

In the subsequent Lomé conventions that deal with development relations between the EU and countries in Africa, the Caribbean and the Pacific (ACP), and in the association agreements with Eastern European countries, reference is made to human rights. The Fourth Lomé Convention which was signed between the European Community and 68 ACP countries in 1989, refers to human rights in its preamble where it states: 'Co-operation shall be directed towards development centred on man, the main protagonist and beneficiary of development, which thus entails respect for and promotion of all human rights.'[6] This text does not provide for the supension of aid or intervention by the European Union in the case of violations of human rights,[7] but it has stimulated the involvement of the European Commission in human rights. The periodic consultations between the EU and the ACP countries often include human rights situations. Lomé IV also provides for the allocation of financial resources for the promotion of human rights in the ACP states that request such aid. In the event of a serious breach of human rights, the Union can denounce the Convention for any ACP country on six months' notice. This has, however, never happened so far.

Following the revision of the Lomé IV Convention, which was finalized at the end of 1995, it now contains, in addition to references to human rights, a suspension clause to be invoked in cases of violation of the essential elements of the Convention. This policy has been confirmed in the

Commission's report on its activities to promote human
rights and democracy, published in July 1995. Positive measures are to be given priority, but the European Union
should intervene in situations of grave violation of human
rights. Its response should always be guided by fair and
equitable criteria, and adjusted to the particular circumstances, but the political dialogue with the country concerned should be maintained wherever possible, while the
local population should not be penalized twice through potential sanctions by the EU. Humanitarian aid and emergency relief should always continue.[8]

Non-governmental organizations have urged the
Commission to be more precise in indicating which human
rights are at issue; the knowledge of the civil servants that
are involved should be expanded; there should be a more
systematic channel of information about what is happening
in the field of human rights in the ACP countries and in
Central America. It now often depends too much on the
personal interest of the commissioner, director-general or
other functionaries that happen to be involved how much
attention is paid to human rights. Usually, the Commission
in cases of gross violations of human rights prefers an approach by 'quiet diplomacy' rather than to criticize the situation in another country in public. An exception is the
situation in Turkey, where – undoubtedly under the
influence of EU-member Greece – relatively much public
pressure has been exerted in response to reported human
rights violations. The EU has expressed concern about the
fate of political prisoners and the restricted role of political
parties during elections. This type of pressure may have
some effect in the case of Turkey, as this country that has a
treaty of association with the EU, has applied for full membership. In 1995, the European Parliament approved a
customs union with Turkey, although some commentators
had questioned the wisdom of doing so in view of continued human rights violations in that country.

The EU has also paid attention to the human rights situation in non-associated states, such as Rwanda and China.[9] Other countries that have been 'punished' by a decrease or temporary suspension of development aid or trade were Haiti, Malawi, Nigeria, Sri Lanka, Sudan and Togo. In some of these cases this has in fact led to an improvement of the human rights situation.

THE EUROPEAN PARLIAMENT

The European Parliament used to have few legislative powers. It still has mainly an advisory, supervisory and consultative role, but after the Maastricht Treaty entered into force, its powers to reject Commission proposals have been considerably strengthened. Treaties of association with third parties must be approved by the Parliament. Its budgetary power deals mainly with the non-obligatory expenses of the Union. Resolutions of the European Parliament are not legally binding, but they do have some political significance. It pays relatively much attention to human rights questions. This happens in the Sub-Committee on Human Rights which is subordinate to the Committee on Foreign Affairs and Security. The Sub-Committee publishes an annual report about human rights in the world and the human rights policy of the Union.

The report for 1993–94[10] dealt with human rights abuses relating to genocide and ethnic cleansing, victims of internal armed conflicts, the development of a right to humanitarian intervention, freedom of expression, rights of minorities, women and children. The report furthermore dealt with the need for the promotion of human rights and democracy as an integral part of EU foreign policy. A striking feature of the report was the reiteration of the principle that EU development aid should be made conditional upon, *inter alia,* the performance of the aid-receiving

country in the area of human rights, democracy and administrative transparency.[11]

In July 1991, the European Parliament adopted a resolution which called for drawing up an annual report on
respect for human rights *within* the Union. The second
such report was presented to the Parliament in December
1994.[12] The report covered such items as torture and ill-
treatment, conditions of detention, freedom of expression,
the rule of law, racism, xenophobia, anti-semitism and discrimination of ethnic minorities, poverty, economic, social
and cultural rights, attacks on asylum-seekers, immigrants,
the handicapped, children, domestic workers from third
countries, trade union rights and privacy. The report, which
was strongly contested and after two plenary debates finally
rejected by the Parliament, also mentioned a number of
country situations, such as the retention of the death
penalty in Belgium (since then abolished), torture and ill-
treatment in Spain, Portugal and Italy, the imprisonment of
conscientious objectors in Greece and the detention of
asylum-seekers in Belgium.[13]

The European Parliament holds debates on human rights
in third countries, when it has to approve cooperation agreements, financial protocols, etc. Recent examples are the
debates, wound up by resolutions, on financial protocols
with Morocco and Syria, the conclusion of a customs union
with Turkey and the human rights crisis in Nigeria after the
execution of political opponents and human rights activists.
The committees of development cooperation and foreign
affairs increasingly debate country dossiers in the presence
of human rights activists from the countries concerned.

In addition, the European Parliament undertakes the
following activities in the field of human rights:

- Public debates which may lead to the adoption of
  resolutions based on specific committee reports. In
  1993, the European Parliament expressed concern

over the resurgence of racism and xenophobia in
Europe and the danger of right-wing extremist violence. Racism and xenophobia should be considered
as matters of 'common interest to the Member States
and thus to require Community actions in support of
and complementary to those of the Member States.'
Other reports on human rights-related matters, recently adopted after public debates, concern the
dealth penalty, conscientious objection to military
service, the situation of gypsies in Europe, harmonization of EU asylum law and policy, poverty and
social exclusion in Europe. Other reports concerned
the political and human rights situation in particular
countries such as Sri Lanka and Sudan.

● Written or oral questions to the Commission and the
Council of Ministers. Questions may concern such
issues as accession by the EU to the European
Convention on Human Rights, the application of the
Lomé Convention or human rights violations in par-
ticular countries.

● Public hearings which are occasionally organized,
such as in 1983 about human rights in Turkey, in
1985 about Iran, in 1990 about Tibet, in February
1993 on the rape of women in the former Yugoslavia,
in June 1993 on human rights and foreign policy
(*inter alia* on the conditionality of development aid)
and in December 1993 on the rehabilitation of
victims of torture.[14] Following the massacre in Dili on
East Timor by Indonesian army units in November
1991, the Parliament's Subcommittee on Human
Rights organized a public hearing on the situation in
East Timor. The hearing was addressed by experts on
the political and historic background and context of
the human rights problems on the island, by representatives of the Timorese political opposition and
human rights organizations, by eye-witnesses and by

relatives of the victims.[15] In November 1995, the European Parliament organized a hearing on the human rights clause in external agreements, with contributions from the EU Commission, human rights activists, academics, and representatives from third countries, which raised the legal, political and economic aspects of the implementation of such clauses.

- Calling attention to human rights during foreign visits; this approach is increasingly made use of. Quite often delegations of the European Parliament pay visits abroad; during these visits the issue of violations of human rights may be raised. Declarations by the European Parliament carry much weight abroad – more than in Europe itself. In Europe, the European Parliament is generally not considered to be politically of great importance, whereas in Latin America, Africa and Asia, members of the European Parliament are seen in the first place as representatives of the economically powerful European Union.

- Interparliamentary delegations and other direct contacts. Making 'discrete démarches' is the term that is often used in this context. The President of the European Parliament may write letters to his national counterparts, to national governments or their ambassadors, and express his concern about the human rights situation in their country. It depends a great deal on the personal attitude of whoever happens to be President to what extent this method is being made use of.

COUNCIL OF MINISTERS

Most of the activities of the EU Ministers in the field of human rights used to take place within the framework of

European Political Cooperation (EPC). This cooperation has existed since 1970 and was formalized in the Single European Act of 1986. In the Act the then twelve European governments endeavoured jointly to formulate and implement a European foreign policy. They undertook 'to inform and consult each other on any foreign policy matters of general interest.' The Act provided for the establishment of a joint secretariat in Brussels to assist the Presidency in the preparation and execution of the activities of EPC. Human rights were mentioned twice in the preamble of the Single European Act. The Act provided a treaty basis for EPC whose character has always remained inter-governmental: EPC decisions required consensus among the member-states. The Maastricht Treaty on European Union, which was adopted by the member-states in February 1992, has given further elaboration to these provisions. The Union and its member-states will define and implement a common foreign and security policy, including human rights. The Common Foreign and Security Policy has taken the place of what used to be European Political Cooperation.

On 21 July 1986, the Foreign Ministers of the EC, meeting in the framework of EPC and the Council, published a Declaration on Human Rights and Foreign Policy. This was renewed and further elaborated in the declaration of 29 June 1991, which emphasized the commitment and even the duty of the member-states to promote human rights worldwide and which outlined positions of the European Community and its member-states on a number of major current policy issues.

The main outlines of common human rights policy, which were then formulated, have been maintained:

- respect for human rights is one of the cornerstones of European identity;
- the protection of human rights is the legitimate and continuous duty of the world community and of all

nations individually, wherever in the world these rights are violated;

- expressions of concern at violations of such rights cannot be considered interference in the domestic affairs of a state;
- the Common Foreign and Security Policy policy is non-selective, without bias to political views or ideology;
- civil and political rights and economic, social and cultural rights are indivisible in character and essential for the full realisation of human dignity;
- the principles of democracy, the rule of law and respect for human rights are closely interconnected;
- the promotion of lasting security and peace between nations cannot be separated from the promotion of the enjoyment of human rights within nations.[16]

Other activities involve:

- emphasis on positive measures to promote human rights and democratic institution building;
- recognition of the need for more coherence and consistency;
- an integrated approach to human rights together with measures to promote good governance and discourage excessive military spending;
- adoption of a standard policy to insert human rights clauses in all EU agreements with third countries.[17]

The Political Committee (CoPo) is the main preparatory organ for the Common Foreign and Security Policy. It consists of the directors-general for political affairs of the ministries of Foreign Affairs as well as a representative of the European Commission. It meets at least once every month. CoPo divides its tasks among a number of working groups that are accountable to it. Since the end of 1987 there exists a special working group on human rights which prepares the general outlines of human rights policy, adopts common positions on human rights issues, and coordinates the activities of the Council of Ministers in the field of human rights. Furthermore, it prepares co-operation in international fora such as the UN General Assembly and the UN Commission on Human Rights. There is also a working group on the Organization on Security and Cooperation in Europe (OSCE) as well as regional working groups which deal with the general political situation, including human rights, in the various geographical regions of the world.

The discussions aim for the exchange of information, the harmonization of policy of the member-states, the preparation of ministerial meetings of the European Council (of government leaders), the request of special reports from the embassies of the member-states or the preparation of demarches. The working groups report either to CoPo or directly to the ministers of Foreign Affairs. Since 1986, the Minister of Foreign Affairs who presides over the Council of Ministers of Foreign Affairs, prepares a memorandum on the EU's activities in the field of human rights, which is sent to the European Parliament. The quality of these memoranda depends very much on the commitment to human rights of the presiding member-state.[18] It is, however, of considerable importance that, due to these periodic reports and through the establishment of the working group on human rights within CoPo, the issue of human rights has acquired a permanent place on the Council's agenda.

Human rights may also come to the Council of Ministers within the framework of its international economic and development policies, for example, when it prepares for a renewal of the Lomé agreements. The resolution on human rights, democracy and development of 28 November 1991 of the European Council of Ministers for Development Co-operation says:

> The Community and its Member States recognize the necessity of a consistent approach towards human rights, democracy and development in their co-operation with third countries. Development co-operation focuses on the central place of the individual and has therefore in essence to be designed with a view to promoting – in parallel with economic and social rights – civil and political liberties by means of a pluralistic, representative democracy that is based on respect for classical rights.[19]

Common European foreign policy deals with such matters as foreign aid, common reactions to human rights violations, the sending of monitors and the extending of formal recognition. The Union has sent its own contingents of human rights observers to such countries as the former Yugoslavia and Rwanda. It tries to make joint contributions to international or regional organizations involved in preventive diplomacy or conflict resolution, as in Central Africa or in Chechnya.[20]

Its role is of increasing importance, but it is by no means that all foreign policy is made in Brussels. The Single European Act and the Maastricht Treaty have reinforced the idea of arriving at a common European foreign policy, but not yet changed the system fundamentally. For the time being, foreign policy – including human rights policy – is still mainly prepared in the national capitals, but the role of the Common Foreign and Security Policy is clearly growing. The forthcoming Inter-Governmental Conference to review the Treaty, which will begin in 1996, is expected to formulate recommendations for a more coherent human rights policy and action as an integral part of the Common Foreign and Security Policy.

THE NATIONAL CAPITALS

It is not feasible to give here a presentation of the human rights policies of all Western European states. Some of them, such as the Scandinavian states and the Netherlands, pay more attention to human rights, partly as a result of pressure by public opinion, than countries such as Belgium or Switzerland. We will limit ourselves to some observations about the role of human rights in the foreign policy of the three major countries of Western Europe: the United Kingdom, France and Germany.[21] The Netherlands is dealt with in a separate chapter (see Chapter 11).

To begin with, Britain and France still – if decreasingly so – try to maintain their former status of major powers in their foreign policy. They are still the only Western European powers that possess nuclear weapons.[22] Moreover, their permanent membership of the UN Security Council provides them with additional prestige. Germany, on the other hand, for a long time carried the vestiges of its Nazi past. However, since the removal of the Berlin Wall and the unification of the two Germanies in 1990, it is gradually regaining its former status of world power.[23] But the gross violations of human rights during the period 1933–45 have not been forgotten in Germany. That gives human rights a special role in present-day German foreign policy, as is illustrated by the following pronouncement by Chancellor Helmut Kohl:

> We Germans have a special obligation, to fight for freedom and human rights – an obligation which finds its foundation in our history. The German people cannot be deprived of this moral attitude for the misdeeds of national-socialist dictatorship. It is expressed in the obligation to make human rights into the standard of our policy.[24]

In this sense Germany is not yet a 'normal' state. Where fundamental human rights were violated so gruesomely by the national-socialists, the German government considers the assertion of human rights – both at home and abroad – a special obligation. The governments of Britain and France are not affected by similar kinds of special obligations; they see themselves as bearing national traditions and continuing the national past. They seem to be less in need than the Germans of international approval of their foreign policy actions.

The foreign policy of the three countries has been strongly determined by developments since 1945. The Second World War meant a change in their former status of major powers to the present one of the middle rank. In the case of Britain and France, the establishment of the North Atlantic Treaty (1949) meant that they henceforth relied on the military protection of the United States; the independent military role of both countries definitively ended with the failure of the Suez operation in 1956.

Through membership of the EEC (1957) France succeeded, together with West Germany, to build for itself a position of economic and political strength in Western Europe. President Charles de Gaulle and his successors attached considerable importance to the symbolism of national independence. France's departure from NATO's military organization (1966) confirmed this symbolism. France henceforth had nominally an independent defence policy, but it was in actual fact closely tied to that of the other western powers.

In 1972 the United Kingdom became a member of the European Economic Community and thereby opted for participation in the economic integration of Europe, at the expense of its economic ties with the Commonwealth. Before that time, it had been forced mainly for financial reasons to give up its military role 'East of Suez'. Henceforth, British military responsibilities were limited to Western Europe and a few isolated territories outside Europe. The war with Argentina over the Falkland Islands

(1982) provided Britain with an opportunity, at the expense of a militarily weak opponent, to make a show of force. The war was ostensibly conducted (by *both* parties) to defend the right to self-determination of the inhabitants of the Falklands, but domestic factors were, certainly in the case of Britain, of crucial importance.[25]

The foreign policy of Germany is, even more than that of Britain and France, determined by the outcome of the Second World War. Crucial events in the postwar period were the founding of the German Federal Republic (1949), West German rearmament and its becoming a member of NATO (1955), EEC membership (1957), the Eastern treaties (1970–72), which normalized its relations with Eastern Europe and membership of the United Nations (1973). The normalization of relations with Eastern Europe included the recognition of the Oder-Neisse border with Poland, the establishment of diplomatic relations with the German Democratic Republic, and finally in 1990 the fall of the Wall and German reunification.

Since the Second World War, the foreign relations of the three countries have been characterized by a large measure of interdependence. Through the greatly improved means of communication there is an almost permanent contact among cabinet ministers and top officials, either through personal meetings or over the telephone. This increased interdependence does not mean, however, that the three governments have given up their claims to national sovereignty. Especially for the benefit of their domestic audiences they continue to stress the national character of the formation of foreign policy. It is not so long ago that the then British Prime Minister, Mrs Thatcher, qualified the importance of European unification and emphasized the continued importance of national sovereignty:

> My first guiding principle is this: willing and active cooperation between independent sovereign states is the best

way to build a successful Europe. To try to suppress na-
tionhood and concentrate power at the centre of a
European conglomerate would be highly damaging and
would jeopardise the objectives we wish to achieve.[26]

In Britain she does not stand alone in her views, as her successor, John Major, has found out when trying to steer the
Maastricht Treaty through the House of Commons.

Next to increased interdependence, there is also a trend
toward increased 'domesticization' of foreign policy: national
parliaments and domestic nonparliamentary groups increasingly try to get a grip on foreign policy. In a certain sense international interdependence and the increased domestic
nature of foreign policy stand at odds with each other.

HUMAN RIGHTS IN BRITISH, FRENCH AND GERMAN FOREIGN POLICY

Human rights is a policy area where domestic factors play
an important role. Domestic groups are active and try to
influence policy. Efforts are made to put pressure on governments 'to do something' about the phenomenon of
human rights violations elsewhere. It is an issue which can
be used by governments as an instrument of foreign policy.
Western governments have used it to criticize the Soviet
Union and its allies as well as certain Third World countries,
including China. The case of South Africa used to be quite
different, as there were important western economic
interests at stake.

Germany

Among the three countries, Germany has most clearly pronounced itself in favour of a foreign policy in which human
rights occupy a central position. Article 1, paragraph 2 of
the German Constitution refers to the 'inviolable and

inalienable human rights as the foundation of every human society, and of peace and justice in the world'. The German Ministry of Foreign Affairs is responsible for the coordination of human rights policy. Within the ministry there does not exist a separate section for human rights. Usually, such matters are dealt with by the division that is responsible for the political aspects of the economic and social activities of the United Nations and the special bureau for the OSCE. The country desks deal with bilateral affairs. Responsibility for the European human rights institutions rests with the Ministry of Justice, which also deals with complaints against Germany in the context of the United Nations and the Council of Europe.[27]

The basic tenets of West German foreign policy have been continued after reunification of the two Germanies. In the words of then Foreign Minister Hans-Dietrich Genscher: 'Considering all that has happened in Germany's past, our country's place at all times can only be on the side of human rights, on the side of the right of self-determination, territorial integrity, and sovereignty of all nations.'[28] The main principles of German human rights policy are based on the rights that are codified in international legal instruments. It considers civil and political rights on the one hand, and economic, social and cultural rights on the other, as 'equal in rank'. Neither deficiencies in social and economic development nor an ideology that is only directed to the attainment of social well-being justify a curtailing of political rights. Because human rights should be respected for all human beings without distinction as to race, sex, language or religion, they must not be split up but remain indivisible. Special attention must be given to the rights of women and children, who are in particular need of protection.

The German government stresses the basic individual nature of human rights. However, it does not rule out the adoption of 'collective rights' or 'rights of the third generation', provided that the contents of these rights can be legally clearly defined and that they are not already covered by existing standards. These existing standards should moreover not be restricted by the adoption of such new rights. The government considers the realisation of the right to self-determination of peoples as a condition for a stable, international order that is based on respect for human rights. This right applies not only to the former colonies, but to all peoples. It should be seen in close connection with the realisation of political and civil rights.[29]

The German government is quite aware of the tension that may arise between the promotion of human rights and the maintenance of friendly relations with foreign governments: 'Support for human rights *vis-à-vis* states that violate human rights may put a considerable burden on bilateral relations. Decisions on specific cases can only be taken within the framework of a more general consideration of interests, in which our engagement for the protection of human rights takes an eminent position.'[30]

For many years Germany has worked on behalf of the abolition of the death penalty in the United Nations. It considers the adoption of the Second Optional Protocol to the Covenant on Civil and Political Rights (1989) as an important result of its efforts. It has ratified most international human rights instruments, but there are also a number of important omissions. Among the conventions that Germany has *not* ratified are: the declaration on individual or group complaints under the Convention against Racial Discrimination, the Convention on the Non-Applicability of Statutory Limitations to War Crimes and Crimes against Humanity, ILO Convention No. 156 concerning Equal Opportunities and Equal Treatment for Men and Women Workers, ILO Convention No. 169 concerning Indigenous People, the Convention for the Suppression of Traffic in Persons, and the Convention on the Protection of the Rights of Migrant Workers. At the World Conference on

Human Rights in Vienna, the German Foreign Minister announced that Germany would henceforth ratify the First Optional Protocol to the International Covenant on Civil and Political Rights. He strongly criticized the acts of violence against foreigners in Germany which he termed a 'disgrace for our country.'[31]

The German government has been criticized for the absence of an apparatus that can call for the involvement of human rights experts, to help to determine priorities in its human rights policies.[32] It has been accused by Amnesty International of ill-treatment of asylum-seekers and other foreign nationals.[33]

France

When the two-hundredth anniversary of the French Revolution was celebrated in 1989, a great deal of attention was devoted to the Declaration on the Rights of Man and the Citizen. It reflects an important tradition in French political life. In the words of former prime minister Raymond Barre: 'A policy that considers itself realistic cannot cut off human rights.'[34]

The French government sees human rights as an important dimension of its foreign policy.[35] Symbolic of that attitude was the fact that the conference on the human dimension of OSCE (see Chapter 4, p. 45) was held in Paris in 1989. French involvement with human rights is further shown by many bilateral and multilateral activities. In 1984 a Consultative Committee for Human Rights was set up to advise the government on the promotion of human rights in the world in general and in international organizations in particular. In 1986, it was attached to the state secretariat for human rights in the office of the prime minister.[36] The Committee consists of 40 members representing major non-governmental organizations, individual experts, members of parliament and ministries.[37]

The French government likes to stress its many interventions on behalf of individual victims of human rights violations. It often prefers an approach of silent diplomacy: 'This has produced important results, taking into account that the confidentiality which is observed constitutes an important factor in the success of these demarches.'[38] In the past, the French Government has often intervened on behalf of victims of human rights in the Soviet Union. This occurred often with reference to individual cases, but the demarches have also dealt with human rights issues of a more general nature. Sometimes sanctions were applied or other measures taken which included the world of sport. France also participated in the states' complaint against Turkey (see Chapter 6, p. 72). At the fortieth anniversary of the Universal Declaration of Human Rights, President Mitterrand expressed his support for the work of nongovernmental organizations in the field of human rights as follows:

> I do not forget the daily stubborn activities of non-governmental organizations, who report on, protest and denounce violations of human rights and give support to the victims of such violations. Without them, traces of the victims would disappear for ever, their rights ridiculed in secret. France will support the consolidation of these activities, the clarification of their position and protect their members, actors and witnesses ...[39]

The French government has, however, been criticized for paying more attention to the faults of others, while disregarding its own deficiencies regarding human rights in France itself and in its overseas territories such as New Caledonia.[40] Amnesty International is among human rights organizations that have criticized France for its treatment of conscientious objectors and has reported on allegations of ill-treatment in police custody, often concerning immigrants and French citizens of North African origin.[41]

Like Germany, France has ratified many, but not all, international human rights treaties. Among the treaties which it has *not* ratified are: the Second Optional Protocol regarding the abolition of the death penalty, ILO Convention No. 169 concerning Indigenous People, the Convention on the Non-Applicability of Statutory Limitations to War Crimes and Crimes against Humanity, the Convention on the Rights of Migrant Workers, the Convention on the Nationality of Married Women, and the Convention on the Consent to Marriage, Minimum Age for Marriage and Registration of Marriages.

The United Kingdom

An official policy paper issued in 1978 mentions concern for human rights explicitly as a goal of Great Britain's foreign policy.[42] It contains lists of possible actions to take in the event of glaring violations of human rights in other countries. The measures range from letters to politicians, through cancellation of ministerial visits, to trading sanctions. Emphasis is put on the need for a general and consistent posture on human rights throughout the world, coupled with the attempt to apply uniform standards. The Foreign and Commonwealth Office should establish a systematic procedure for judging each country's human rights performance each year. This has not led the British government to publish a British version of the annual US State Department Reports, but it has said repeatedly that human rights are a matter of legitimate international concern. It has asserted for itself the right to make judgements and the duty to accept that its own actions may come under scrutiny, according to Parliamentary Under-Secretary for Foreign and Commonwealth Affairs, Tim Eggar.[43] At the World Conference on Human Rights in Vienna (June 1993) the British government expressed itself strongly in favour of the universal nature of human rights, while rejecting the notion of 'regional particularities' to

justify depriving people of their human rights. It stressed the
interdependence of human rights and economic development and rejected the notion that the latter should have priority over the former. It also stressed the importance of the
work of non-governmental organizations, 'often the best and
sometimes the only friend of those who suffer from human
rights abuse'.[44]

As in the case of other western governments, for a long
time British human rights policy largely coincided with its
policies toward Eastern Europe. The Foreign Secretary, on
visits to Eastern European countries, would raise, whenever
possible and sometimes to the embarrassment of his hosts,
particular human rights cases and the general human rights
situation in the country he was visiting.[45] However, from
1985 onwards, Mrs Thatcher developed a very positive attitude toward Mikhail Gorbachev as 'a man with whom we
can do business'. Since 1989, the British government has re-
oriented human rights emphases into a North/South dimension, with an explicit emphasis on 'good governance',
especially in its relations with African countries. It has been
reluctant to criticize China's human rights record, because
of the sensitivity of the Hong Kong issue.

The British government has often been criticized for its
domestic human rights policies, especially in regard to its
actions against members of the Irish Republican Army.[46] A
long-time criticism has been that the government has not
issued clear directives for weighing human rights concerns
against other interests in its foreign policy: '[S]ome sense of
priorities more certain than predictions on who is most
likely to win a battle in the Cabinet would seem on the face
of it to be desirable.'[47] Subsequent British cabinets have not
shown much inclination to prepare a public document on
the place of human rights in its foreign policy, along the
lines of, for instance, the Dutch memorandum of 1979.

The United Kingdom has acceded to major international
human rights treaties, but there remains a sizable number

which it has *not* yet ratified. Among these are: the two optional protocols to the International Covenant on Civil and Political Rights, ILO Convention No. 111 concerning Discrimination in Respect of Employment and Occupation, No. 156 on Equal Opportunities and Equal Treatment for Men and Women Workers, No. 169 on Indigenous People, the Convention on the Non-Applicability of Statutory Limitations to War Crimes and Crimes against Humanity, the Convention for the Suppression of Traffic in Persons and the International Convention on the Protection of the Rights of Migrant Workers.

CONCLUSION

Human rights policy of the West European states that belong to the European Union, has increasingly become a matter of concern for the Common Foreign and Security Policy. The matter is also receiving increasing attention from the European Commission; witness the appointment in early 1993 of a separate Commissioner to deal with common foreign policy matters. Both within the directorates of the European Union and within the Council of Ministers, permanent officials are now charged with the preparation and execution of a common human rights policy. This is especially evident in the relations with the ACP countries that are associated with the EU. The fourth Lomé agreement provides for a certain measure of reciprocity, which may eventually lead to raising human rights matters *within* EU territory – which so far has happened only rarely. The European Parliament is showing increasing concern with issues of human rights, both within and outside the EU.

In Western European countries a certain degree of domesticization of foreign policy can be observed. As long as human rights is in keeping with other goals, governments

tend to use it as an instrument of foreign policy. It thus
used to fit well in the confrontation policy with the Soviet
Union. In this regard the policy of the major Western
European states did not differ from that of the United
States. When economic interests are at stake, however, as
used to be the case with South Africa, the West Europeans
have shown themselves more reluctant to act than their
American colleagues.

Acting in the framework of Common Foreign and
Security Policy must be considered to be more effective
than isolated actions by national governments. It stands to
reason that statements on behalf of the Fifteen will carry
more weight than démarches by one state acting on its
own.[48] It also serves as a 'shield' for governments to ward
off being singled out by a government that has been condemned for its human rights record.[49] However, reaching
consensus among the Fifteen sometimes goes at the
expense of clarity of views to be expressed. The need for
compromise may lead to rather colourless, bland statements. Another problem is the lack of effective parliamentary control over negotiations within the framework of the
Common Foreign and Security Policy. The latter problem
can only be solved if the European Parliament is provided
with the real powers of control it has always been asking for.
On that score, most of the member-states have shown themselves very reluctant, however.[50] This means that, for the
time being, common foreign policy still lacks effective
democratic control.

10 The Third World

The greater part of the world's population lives in what usually is called the 'Third World', the countries in Asia, Africa and Latin America, also called the 'developing world'. It would be impossible to present in one chapter a full treatment of the relevance of human rights for the foreign policy of all of these countries. This chapter will do no more than give a rough summary of what these countries have in common as far as human rights in their foreign policy is concerned.

BACKGROUND

To the extent that human rights are concerned with the protection of the rights of the individual, they reflect what are commonly seen as western values. But even if – as is sometimes argued – human rights are not only of western origin, there can be little doubt that in their written form the freedom rights particularly can be traced to western authors.

The American political scientist Jack Donnelly has argued that although human rights are western in origin they are of nearly universal contemporary relevance: 'Contemporary social conditions have given the idea and practice of human rights wide applicability.'[1] The greater emphasis on rights of the community rather than of the individual distinguishes these countries in culture and philosophy from western countries.[2] There is often little understanding for western individualism, which is often even explicitly rejected. In Africa, concern for the rights of the individual is almost exclusively recognized within existing social, economic and cultural dimensions.[3] In the case of Islamic countries, moreover, certain internationally recognized human rights are considered to be contrary to fundamental norms

133

of the Islam.[4] In some Islamic countries there exist strong differences of view about what constitutes human rights. In this connection it should be stressed that, according to the Islam, *obligations* must receive more emphasis than *rights*. In the concept for a Universal Islamic Declaration of Human Rights (1981) it is formulated as follows: 'by the terms of our primeval covenant with God our duties and obligations have priority over our rights'.

COLONIALISM

Almost all independent states in the Third World are former European colonies. The colonial experience has for many years influenced the policy – and especially the policy pronouncements – of government leaders of these countries. Many of these pronouncements – including those referring to human rights – can only be understood if they are related to the colonial past. Colonialism is, quite understandably, seen as a denial of the equivalence of all human beings, and thereby of human rights. That is the main reason why Third World countries keep emphasizing that the right to self-determination is not an ordinary right, but the first of these rights.[5] Until not very long ago, colonialism and racial discrimination were about the only violations of human rights which were accepted as such by many African leaders.[6] This also explains the great emphasis which has always been put on combating South Africa's apartheid policy. They regarded apartheid not only as an unjust and wicked system, but also as an affront to the dignity of the African.[7] The Canadian political scientist Rhoda Howard has made the point that civil and political rights in the present sense did not exist in the colonies. Thus preventive detention – which is practised by a number of African governments against their political opponents – is a direct heritage from the colonial past.[8] In short, during the time of colonialism the West has been noted for its human rights violations in its colonies. Racial discrimination, forced labour, expropriation and exploitation of cheap labour were quite common in the colonies. There was a fundamental inequality in the legal and social treatment of whites and non-whites. Oppressive rulers in the Third World like to use the argument of colonialism if for instance western governments accuse them of violating human rights. Western countries – so the argument goes – when making such accusations are guilty of neocolonialism and paternalism, and of meddling in the internal affairs of independent nations. In fact, however, the opposite is true: western countries would be guilty of paternalism if they did *not* apply international human rights standards to the Third World. As the late Evan Luard used to argue, human rights are about the elementary right of people not to be killed, not to be tortured, not be arbitrarily imprisoned, not to be raped or assaulted.[9] There is no reason why such rights should not equally apply to the people of the Third World.

ECONOMIC SELF-DETERMINATION

For many years Third World countries have argued in favour of the establishment of a New International Economic Order (NIEO). This would give them a greater share in natural global wealth, more access to technological knowledge, a moratorium on, or cancellation of, their foreign debts and more multilateral financial assistance. The sixth special session (1973) of the General Assembly of the United Nations asked specifically for such an NIEO. The following year, over the objections of the developed nations, the General Assembly accepted a programme of action, which included expansion of producers' organizations after the model of the Organization of Petroleum Exporting Countries (OPEC), linking prices of imports in developing countries to export prices, reform of the international monetary system, and free exercise of full permanent sovereignty over natural resources (which implied the right of nationalization). The latter right is also contained in the two international human rights covenants adopted in 1966: 'All peoples may, for their own ends, freely dispose of

their natural wealth and resources'.[10] That can mean nationalization or transfer of those resources from foreign
ownership to a developing country's own subjects.

THE RIGHT TO DEVELOPMENT

The term 'right to development' was coined by the
Senegalese member of the International Court of Justice,
Keba M'Baye. All fundamental rights and freedoms, according to M'Baye, are necessarily linked with the right to existence, with a higher standard of living and therefore with
development. The right to development belongs to human
rights, because human beings cannot exist without it.

Since 1979 various UN bodies have tried to formulate a
somewhat satisfactory definition of the right to development. The developing nations were much in favour of this
right, the West European states were divided, while the
United States was strongly opposed. At the end of 1986 the
UN General Assembly adopted, with one opposing vote (the
United States), a Declaration on the Right to
Development.[11] It defines the right to development as an inalienable human right by virtue of which every human
person and all peoples are entitled to participate in, contribute to, and enjoy economic, social, cultural and political
development, in which all human rights and fundamental
freedoms can be fully realized. In the Declaration the *indivisibility* of all human rights is emphasized; equal attention
should be given to the implementation, promotion and protection of civil, political, economic, social and cultural
rights. The maintenance of international peace and security, and even disarmament, is included in the right to development. This has caused extra irritation among its
opponents, especially the Americans. The right to development is, to say the least, a controversial human right.[12]
However, the fact that there are more than one billion
people in the world who can barely survive and who live in
absolute poverty – undernourished, lacking access to health
services, lacking adequate housing, without primary or

secondary education[13] – points to the need for adequate provisions. That means, in the first place, respect for so-called 'basic rights': the right to life, to adequate food, clothing, housing and medical care; and in addition, the right to personal security, freedom of thought, conscience and religion. Other rights of fundamental importance for the people of the Third World are: the right to education; the right to take part in cultural life and to enjoy the benefits of scientific progress and its application; freedom of expression; the right to freedom of association and assembly (including the right to establish free trade unions). All of these rights form part of the right to development.

The Declaration on the Right to Development is not legally binding. Such legally binding formulations are, however, contained in the International Covenant on Economic, Social and Cultural Rights (art. 11) and in the African Charter on Human and Peoples' Rights:

> All peoples shall have the right to their economic, social and cultural development with due regard to their freedom and identity and in the equal enjoyment of the common heritage of mankind.
>
> States shall have the duty, individually or collectively, to ensure the exercise of the right to development.[14]

The fact that the richer countries in the world have for many years considered it a part of their policy to give development aid to poorer nations, may be seen as another indication for the existence of a right to development, if not a right to development *assistance*. The donor countries are faced with a dilemma if aid-receiving governments are found guilty of gross and systematic violations of fundamental human rights. Does that constitute sufficient reason to suspend aid to such a government? At the second World Conference on Human Rights, which was held in Vienna in June 1993, many of the governments of developing nations rejected the idea of linking the giving of development aid to the human rights performance of aid-receiving countries. In the words of the Foreign Minister of Indonesia, Ali Alatas:

Human rights are vital and important by and for themselves. So are efforts at accelerated national development,
especially of the developing countries. Both should be
vigorously pursued and promoted. Indonesia, therefore,
cannot accept linking questions of human rights to economic and development cooperation, by attaching human
rights implementation as political conditionalities to such
cooperation. Such a linkage will only detract from the
value of both.[15]

The case of Indonesia is of particular interest, as in 1992
it rejected further development aid from the Netherlands
because of 'the reckless use of development assistance as an
instrument of intimidation or as a tool for threatening
Indonesia'. (In a reaction to major human rights violations
by the Indonesian army, the Netherlands had suspended
its development aid to Indonesia – see further in
Chapter 11.)

PEOPLES' RIGHTS

Third World governments tend to stress peoples' rights, for
example with respect to the right to self-determination, the
right to natural resources and the right to development.
Article 1 of both International Covenants of 1966 refers to
the 'rights of peoples to self-determination'. A more recent
development is the current discussion about the rights of
indigenous peoples.
    The notion of 'peoples' rights' received further public
recognition with the adoption of a Universal Declaration of
the Rights of Peoples by a conference of independent
experts in Algiers in 1976.[16] Although the term 'peoples'
was not defined, it corresponded closely to the notion of
'state'.[17] The African Charter of Human and Peoples'
Rights contains a number of articles which explicitly
mention the rights of peoples.[18] That document does not
define the concept, either. Next to the right to self-
determination peoples are granted the right to equality
('All peoples shall be equal'), the right to existence and the

right to liberation. It has been suggested that the title of the African Charter ('Human Rights *and* Peoples' Rights') indicates that a peoples' right is by itself not a human right, but rather an addition to it.[19] Others see peoples' rights as a subcategory of human rights.[20]

So far, there does not exist a commonly accepted definition of what exactly constitutes a 'people'. A definition would most likely include at least the following elements:[21]

- a number of human beings forming a group, the size of which would seem to vary greatly;
- the group distinguishes itself from other groups by certain cultural traits which the members of the group hold in common, such as language, religion, history, and certain national symbols;
- often the group seeks to preserve or to achieve recognition in the form of political autonomy or independence.

Though most Third World countries emphasize the right to self-determination of peoples, they tend to reject secession. The government of India, for example, made an explicit reservation when it ratified the International Convenants of 1966 by declaring that the right to self-determination only referred to 'peoples under foreign domination' and not to sovereign independent states or to a section of a people or nation – which is the essence of national integrity'.[22] The exact meaning of 'foreign domination' remains very much a matter of interpretation. Many members of the Sikh community consider themselves to be under foreign (i.e. Indian) domination. The same is true for the Kurds, the Palestinians and the Basques. Recognition of their right to self-determination would be at the expense of the territories of existing states. Those states commonly reject such an interpretation of self-determination. They prefer to maintain the national borders as determined at the time of gaining independence. Most governments of Third World countries find that self-determination should not affect the territorial integrity of their state.

Also unsolved is the question of how representatives of peoples should be chosen. In 1991, a non-governmental organization was established to promote the interests of non-recognized peoples: the 'Unrepresented Nations and Peoples Organization' (UNPO) which has struggled with similar problems. In its covenant a Nation or People is defined as 'a group of human beings which possesses the will to be identified as a nation or people and to determine its common destiny as a nation or people, and is bound by a common heritage which can be historical, racial, ethnic, linguistic, cultural, or territorial'.[23] A special feature of UNPO is that prospective members must reject totalitarianism and religious intolerance as well as terrorism as an instrument of policy.[24]

The question of whether a certain group of people is considered a 'people' depends usually more on the results of internal or external wars or the preferences of the great powers than on clear criteria.[25] As long as that is the case, peoples' rights will remain very much a weapon in the political debate. Thus its application is likely for the time being to remain more a matter of might than a matter of right.

INDIGENOUS RIGHTS

In international organs increasing attention is being paid to the rights of indigenous peoples who consider themselves oppressed by (white) settlers who militarily occupied their lands, which they used to have entirely to themselves, and who systematically assaulted their ways of life. The entering into treaties, as many North American Indian tribes did with the governments of the United States and Canada, has made little difference in terms of the discrimination and land seizures to which they have been subjected.[26] In 1957 the International Labour Organization adopted Convention No. 107 concerning the Protection and Integration of Indigenous and Other Tribal and Semi-Tribal Populations in Independent Countries, which was revised in 1989 (Convention No. 169). Since 1977 the UN Sub-Commission on the Prevention of Discrimination and the

Protection of Minorities has studied the issue and since 1982 a special Working Group has been charged with the problem. It concluded its work on a draft declaration on the rights of indigenous peoples in 1994. It was adopted by the Sub-Commission in the same year and is now under consideration by the Commission on Human Rights.[27]

So far, no agreement exists with regard to a common definition of the term 'indigenous peoples', who are sometimes referred to as the 'Fourth World'.[28] One of the main reasons for this failure is that the terminology embraces groups of people who have very little in common.[29] Most often used is the definition provided in 1983 by José Martinez Cobo, the Special Rapporteur of the UN Sub-Commission:

> Indigenous communities, peoples and nations are those which, having a historical continuity with pre-invasion and pre-colonial societies that developed on their territories, consider themselves distinct from other sectors of the societies now prevailing in those territories, or parts of them. They form at present non-dominant sectors of society and are determined to preserve, develop and transmit to future generations their ancestral territories, and their ethnic identity, as the basis of their continued existence as peoples, in accordance with their own cultural patterns, social institutions and legal systems.[30]

Groups such as the American Indians, the Inuit (Eskimo) and Aleutians of the circumpolar region, the Sami (Lapps) of northern Europe, the Aborigines and Torres Strait Islanders of Australia, and the Maori of New Zealand are commonly understood as indigenous.[31]

The World Conference on Human Rights held in Vienna in June 1993 paid special attention to indigenous people. Among other things it recommended that the General Assembly should proclaim an international decade of the world's indigenous people to begin in 1994, including action-orientated programmes to be decided upon in partnership with indigenous people. To the disappointment of many of the non-governmental organizations, it decided *not* to use the term 'indigenous peoples' (with an 's' at the end of the word), as this might give the connotation of a recognition of political claims, which many states want to avoid.

Apart from the terminology, other so far unsolved problems relate to the question of representation: there are no international rules as to how indigenous people should elect or appoint their representatives to international meetings such as those organized by the United Nations. In fact, anybody can claim to represent the interests of indigenous people. Another problem is the question of whether indigenous people should have special rights. Full self-determination, in the sense of complete independence from the dominating people and government, seems hardly possible. Therefore most leaders of indigenous people speak of seeking a degree of self-determination within existing states.[32]

The issue is receiving increased international attention, as symbolized by the award of the Nobel Peace Prize to Rigoberta Menchu, defender of the rights of the indigenous people of Guatemala. The restitution of land to the original people in Colombia and increased interest in the problems and position of indigenous people in Canada and New Zealand are other indications that the issue is being concentrated on.[33]

AFRICA

In the past, African states have been reluctant to make clear pronouncements regarding violations of human rights in other African states, except in the case of South Africa. The Charter of the Organization of African Unity (OAU) is based on the principle of non-intervention in the domestic affairs of states.[34] The gross violations of human rights by the regimes of Amin in Uganda, Nguema in Equatorial Guinea and Bokassa in the Central African Republic led, however, to greater activity by the OAU.[35] In 1981 it adopted the African Charter for Human and Peoples' Rights which came into force in 1986. It has now been ratified by 49 states which means that almost all African states have become parties to the Charter.

We have already discussed, in Chapter 6, the provisions in the African Charter for monitoring human rights. The preamble to the Charter takes into consideration 'the virtues of ... historical tradition and the values of African civilization which should inspire and characterize their reflection on the concept of human and peoples' rights'. One of those specific African traditions is the emphasis on peoples' rights, which was discussed in a previous paragraph. The enjoyment of rights and freedoms is explicitly related to the performance of duties by every person to his family and society, the state and other legally recognized communities and the international community. The preamble also mentions the duties of the states parties to achieve the total liberation of Africa and to undertake to eliminate colonialism, neo-colonialism and apartheid. The elimination of zionism is explicitly mentioned in this list.

The civil and political rights named in the Charter are roughly the same as those contained in the UN Covenant. The African Charter, however, does *not* include the prohibition of involuntary marriage, it does not limit the death penalty to the most serious crimes, there is no non-derogation provision of the Genocide Convention, no right to seek pardon or commutation of a death sentence, and no prohibition of imprisonment of those who have been sentenced merely because they were unable to fulfill a contractual obligation. In these respects the African Charter is less radical than the UN Covenant on Civil and Political Rights. On the other hand, it goes further than other human rights treaties in that it does not contain any reference to derogation from obligations in times of public emergency. The absence of such a provision is very important, because of the existence in many African states of a more or less permanent state of emergency.[36] Restrictions on the rights mentioned in the Charter are only possible if provided by law. That can mean that the exercise of rights may be substantially limited. Furthermore, the Charter contains provisions about the right to property – which may only be encroached upon 'in the interest of public need or in the interest of the community and in accordance with the

provisions of appropriate laws'; the right to work; the right
to 'enjoy the best attainable state of physical and mental
health'; the right to education; and the right to take part in
the cultural life of the community. These provisions –
except for the right to property – are grafted on similar
provisions in the UN Covenant on Economic, Social and
Cultural Rights.

Much has been written about the shortcomings of the
Charter and its application.[37] The African political scientists
Ojo and Sesay have pointed to the state-centric character
which leads to the question of whether individual rights are
sufficiently protected.[38] The possibilities for individuals to
lodge complaints before the African Commission on
Human Rights are very limited and the ultimate decision as
to whether a complaint will be dealt with rests with the
heads of states and governments.[39] The procedure of reporting by states parties to the Charter needs to be improved.[40] Moreover, the states could use the 'duties' spelt
out in articles 27–29 to derogate rights under the Charter.[41]
The Commission does not have any powers of enforcing its
own decisions. 'Peoples' rights' can be used to limit the
rights of individuals. In the words of Ojo and Sesay: 'Given
the lack of sanctions by the Commission and the OAU itself,
there is nothing to discourage a determined African leader
from obstructing the Commission's work'.[42] They were not
very optimistic when they published their article (1986),
and developments since then would seem to have vindi-
cated their judgement.

Nevertheless, it is still quite important that by adopting
the Charter the African states have provided a translation of
universal human rights standards for the African context.
Thereby they have demonstrated that human rights are not
only a concept that is imposed by the West, but that these
are *their* human rights as well.[43] The Charter should therefore be seen mainly as a symbol rather than as an effective
instrument to protect human rights. Moreover, it is used by
non-governmental organizations, both within and outside
Africa, to remind African governments of the standards
they are supposed to respect.[44] Thus, for example, the

Secretary-General of Amnesty International (Pierre Sané, who happens to be an African himself) has asked the OAU Assembly to end thirty years of silence on human rights violations in Africa and to adopt a programme for action to promote and protect human rights.[45] The need for a proper OAU structure to deal with issues of human rights would also help to improve the relationship between the OAU, which has its permanent secretariat in Addis Ababa, Ethiopia, and the African Commission for Human Rights, which is located in Banjul, The Gambia, at the other end of the continent.[46]

ASIA

The political and cultural cohesion of the countries in Asia is less than that of those on other continents. An indication of this is the absence of a regional international organization that covers the whole of Asia. Asia is a conglomerate of countries with differing social structures and divergent religious, philosophical and cultural traditions.[47]

In the field of human rights, also, Asia shows little homogeneity. One can conceive of a Chinese, a Hindu or a Moslem tradition in human rights,[48] but there is hardly anything that can be called an Asian tradition, linking such countries as divergent as China, Japan, India, Pakistan, Iran, Iraq and others. There is no regional treaty of human rights for Asia. Efforts were made to create a West Asian or a Southeast Asian declaration of human rights, so far with little success. Representatives of non-governmental organizations have set up a 'Regional Council for Human Rights in Asia', which has developed a declaration of basic duties of peoples and governments of the ASEAN countries. (ASEAN is a framework for regional mainly economic co-operation of six Southeast Asian states.) In 1993 these countries decided to appoint a regional rapporteur for human rights. The Charter for Human and Peoples' Rights in the Arab World is not a governmental document but written by individual experts. Asian non-governmental organizations

would seem to have progressed further in this field than
the governments. During the preparation for the World
Conference on Human Rights in Vienna certain governments, including those of China, India, Malaysia, Singapore
and Indonesia, showed some greater degree of coherence,
but that was more to counter what they considered undue
western efforts to press for more effective human rights
monitoring by UN and other organs. The 'Bangkok
Declaration', which resulted from a regional meeting held
in the spring of 1993, was widely interpreted as negative on
the issue of the universal character of human rights, as is
illustrated by the following quotation:

> *Recognize* that while human rights are universal in nature,
> they must be considered in the context of a dynamic and
> evolving process of international norm-setting, bearing in
> mind the significance of national and regional particular-
> ities and various historical, cultural and religious back-
> grounds.[49]

During the World Conference itself the delegates from a
number of Asian countries were seen to be active in trying
to block progress toward strengthening supervision procedures rather than in furthering progress.[50]

In recent years, an increasing number of Asian states has
ratified the international human rights instruments. Nineteen
Asian states have ratified the International Covenants on Civil
and Political Rights and on Economic, Social and Cultural
Rights, while twenty-two have not yet done so. Only Kyrgystan,
Mongolia, Nepal, the Philippines, the Seychelles and South
Korea have ratified the First Optional Protocol regarding the
individual right of complaint.

The countries of the Asian continent are struggling with
enormous problems – including those in the field of human
rights. These include issues relating to civil and political,
economic and social rights, as well 'third generation' rights.
Examples are the pollution of the national environment, as
well as the role of multinational enterprises with regard to
self-determination and sovereignty over natural resources,
and the right to cultural identity.[51]

LATIN AMERICA

The political independence of most countries of Latin America is much older than that of the other countries in the Third World. Thus Latin America was from the beginning involved in the establishment of the Charter of the United Nations and the Universal Declaration of Human Rights. In their foreign policy most Latin American governments used to accept the leadership of the United States of America. This changed with the coming to power of Fidel Castro in Cuba in 1959, which was followed by the victory of the Sandinistas in Nicaragua in 1979. Since then, most Latin American nations have adopted a more independent foreign policy line, but their relationship to the United States has remained a major issue in the foreign policy of most Latin American states.

Most Latin American states are members of the Organization of American States (OAS). The Charter of that organization proclaims as one of its principles the fundamental rights of the individual without distinction as to race, nationality, creed or sex.[52]

The American Declaration on the Rights and Duties of Man was adopted in 1948, shortly before the Universal Declaration of Human Rights.[53] The American Convention on Human Rights (Treaty of San José) was adopted in 1969 and came into force in 1978.[54] Most states on the American continent – with the United States as a notable exception[55] – have acceded to the Convention. The Convention contains the major civil and political rights including the right to life, freedom from torture, personal liberty, fair trial, privacy, nationality, participation in government, equal and judicial protection. The Convention prohibits slavery, and proclaims freedom of conscience and religion, freedom of thought and expression, freedom of movement and residence, freedom of association. States parties to the Convention are obliged to respect these rights and to ensure their free and full exercise. The list of rights is more extensive than that of other human rights treaties, including the European Convention on Human Rights and

Fundamental Freedoms. In 1988 an additional protocol
(Protocol of San Salvador) was adopted relating to economic, social and cultural rights.[56]

Some of the provisions of the American Convention are
so advanced that doubt has been expressed as to whether
there is any country on the American continent that is in
full compliance with all of them.[57] That does not alter the
fact that by the adoption of the Convention a system of
human rights standards has been codified with which governments can be confronted. The Convention contains important provisions for the supervision of respect for human
rights, which we have already touched upon in Chapter 6.[58]

Of all parts of the Third World the American continent
has the most extensive regional system of standards on
human rights. As more experience is gained with procedures of supervision, it will be possible to judge its effectiveness as compared with that of the United Nations itself. In
the past, many gross violations of human rights have occurred in Latin America, especially in the field of extra-
judicial executions, torture and disappearances.[59] In more
recent years, the situation has improved. The system of the
American Convention can contribute to the maintenance
of that improvement.

CONCLUSION

As we said at the outset of this chapter, it is hardly possible
to provide general conclusions about a field as large, as
populated and as varied as 'the Third World'. Such conclusions must remain somewhat vague and speculative. More
precise pronouncements must be reserved for specific
regions or countries.

Nevertheless, the countries of the Third World have some
common characteristics in their human rights policies. For
instance, there is the greater emphasis on collective and
economic and social rights than on civil and political rights.
The colonial past and large-scale poverty and economic
distress are the main reasons for this, but there are also

cultural traditions in which the role of the individual is less pronounced than in western countries.

Closely connected to this is the emphasis that is put on *duties* as well as rights. In societies in which the individual is not number one, it is fitting that he is told of the duties he has *vis-à-vis* society. Therein lurks the danger that the political leaders will abuse this and employ these duties *at the expense* of the rights of the individual. That usually means violations of human rights.

Linked to these two characteristics is the emphasis that is put on the creation of a New International Economic Order and the right to development. Obviously, these factors are more significant in the Third World than in the rich, industrialized West. It is less obvious why western countries have opposed the realization of these rights. Arguments that are advanced are (i) the fact that the right of development was always presented as a right of 'peoples', i.e. of states rather than of individuals; (ii) the right would be used to legitimize an increase in development aid to governments in the South; (iii) too much emphasis on the right to development might be at the expense of the promotion of civil and political rights. However, on the basis of considerations of enlightened self-interest in the long run in stable world politics and a healthy world economy, the realization of a right to development for *all* countries is tremendously important.

The right to political as well as economic self-determination is given much attention in the Third World. In the previous paragraphs we noted the role that a colonial past has played. The concept of 'national self-determination' contains a number of shortcomings which make it hard to apply.

This chapter has shown that the development of a regional system of human rights norms is furthest developed in Latin America. In Africa, a beginning has been made. In Asia, hardly. That difference is partly explained by the divergent cultural cohesion of the countries and the peoples who live on these continents.

11 The Netherlands[1]

The Netherlands is a small Western European nation of 15 million inhabitants that covers an area of 41,000 square kilometers (16,000 square miles). Such a small nation generally lacks the power resources to bring pressure to bear on other states. Whatever influence it may have in international relations must therefore be based on persuasion rather than power.[2]

Dutch foreign policy has been likened to a struggle between the clergyman and the merchant: while wanting to do good all over the world, commercial interests are never lost sight of. In the early 1960s, in certain Dutch political circles it was customary to describe the Netherlands as a *gids-land*, a 'guiding country' that was expected to provide guidance to the world. Cynics like to point out, however, that in the end it is usually commerce that tends to predominate. The prevalence of international trade on the one hand, and a strong attachment to principles of international law on the other, have always been main features of Dutch foreign policy. In modern times, this has found expression in an emphasis on issues of development cooperation and respect for human rights.[3] In his study of Dutch foreign policy, Joris Voorhoeve has distinguished three main traditions: maritime commercialism, neutralist abstentionism, and internationalism.[4] Human rights policy clearly belongs to the last category. This tradition, which also encompasses international development cooperation, has gained increasing importance after the loss of the Dutch colonial empire. The emphasis on human rights and development cooperation is not limited to one political strand in Dutch society. Sometimes it is almost amusing to see how authors of different political colour have claimed human rights as typical of their particular political philosophy. Governments consisting of various party coalitions have given equal attention to the theme of human rights in their foreign policy.

Although the Netherlands is not of course the only country that puts emphasis on human rights in its foreign policy,[5] it is sometimes mentioned as an example to be followed by other nations: witness the following quotation from Norwegian human rights activist Jan Egeland:

> The Netherlands has probably become the most effective human rights advocate today, because she ambitiously combines her favourable image as small state with allocating considerable resources to the planning, implementation and follow-up to an innovative and ambitious policy.... In the UN Human Rights Commission, the General Assembly and other UN bodies, the Dutch are always in the forefront in initiating new substantive mechanisms to monitor, mediate or improve when human rights problems are on the international agenda.[6]

In this chapter we shall ask to what extent this flattering picture is true and what are its consequences.

BASIC DOCUMENTS

A policy memorandum was issued in 1979, in which the government set out the principles of Dutch human rights policy.[7] The Memorandum consists of four parts. The Introduction (Part I) discusses the characteristics of the concept of human rights and gives a survey of the historical development of human rights as a subject of national and international norms. Part II describes the place of human rights in the United Nations, in the Council of Europe, in regional systems outside Europe and in non-governmental organizations. Part III analyses human rights policy for the following subjects: the ends and means of Dutch human rights policy; the relationship between classic and social human rights; development cooperation; the East–West relations; and problems of international communication. Part IV contains 55 policy conclusions.

Through this Memorandum the Dutch government made an effort to present the major dilemmas faced by a government that wants to give human rights a central position in its foreign policy. The Netherlands and Norway[8] seem so far to have been the only countries to publish such an extensive policy document. This Memorandum, which evoked many reactions from non-governmental organizations and which was extensively debated in Parliament, still forms the basis of Dutch human rights policy. Since then, the Foreign Minister has sent two follow-up memoranda to Parliament, which basically confirmed the outlines of the 1979 paper.[9] However, in 1994–95 a major review of Dutch foreign policy took place in which relatively little attention was paid to human rights. This led to expressions of concern by Dutch human rights organization, after which the Foreign ,Minister announced the creation of a new human rights unit within the ministry.

HUMAN RIGHTS AS PART OF OVERALL FOREIGN POLICY

The government emphasized its commitment to human rights as part of its overall foreign policy in the following words:

> The Government regards the promotion of human rights as an essential element of its foreign policy. At the same time it is aware that the implementation of this policy aim raises many difficult problems. Partly those problems stem from the necessity of co-ordinating the promotion of human rights in foreign policy with the promotion of other values and interests the Government has to care for.[10]

Thus the government made clear that it considered human rights as a part of its overall policy, which meant, however, that those rights could not under *all* circumstances enjoy priority. Furthermore, in this and other government documents the following ideas for setting priorities were presented. Joint actions with like-minded countries were to be preferred (though the notion of 'like-mindedness' was not closely defined). Economic measures might only be adopted if other means to improve the human rights situation in another country had proved to be inadequate and the measures would not damage Dutch interests disproportionately. Human rights policy should be 'impartial' and 'non-selective'; that is to say, it must not concentrate on abuses of one particular political colour.

Nevertheless, there would be more reason to make the views of the Netherlands known to countries with which it had historical, cultural and political ties. Development assistance should not be used as a means of manipulation of aid-receiving countries, or in other words, not be offered as a reward for respecting human rights or to punish countries which disregarded these rights. In cases where abuses derive directly from government policy, care should be taken to ensure that aid does not contribute directly to the perpetuation of repression. In cases of gross and persistent violations of fundamental human rights, non-allocation or suspension of aid could be considered.

The Netherlands has stated that it does not want to use development cooperation as an instrument for 'manipulating' recipient countries. In the words of the 1979 Memorandum:

> The Government rejects the idea that aid should be used to reward countries which respect human rights and conversely withheld to punish countries which disregard those rights. Aid should relate to the needs of the people and not to the conduct of governments. Only on this basis can development aid contribute properly to the promotion of human rights, both social and classic.
>
> In cases where abuses derive directly from government policy, one should take care at any rate to ensure that aid does not contribute directly to the perpetuation of repression. Where there is gross and persistent violation of fundamental human rights, non-allocation or suspension of aid can be considered, but other relevant policy considerations must be taken into account before such exceptional measures are taken.[11]

Since 1979 the Dutch Government has declared on various occasions that human rights are a 'central' or 'essential' element of its foreign policy. In the explanatory memorandum to the budget proposals for 1996, the Minister of Foreign Affairs wrote:

> The Government will remain dedicated to human rights. In this respect it sees itself supported by broad domestic support. It will also continue to support processes of democratization, because a democratic legal order is the best guarantee for respect of civil liberties.[12]

Although the Dutch government on many occasions has stated its commitment to economic and social rights, traditionally the main emphasis lies on classical civil and political rights. Within the latter category such issues as torture, involuntary disappearances, and more recently the issue of impunity for human rights offenders have received a relatively large amount of attention.

ORGANISATIONAL STRUCTURE

The organisational structure of the Foreign Ministry reflects the emphasis on human rights. Within the Directorate-General for International Co-operation (DGIS) there is a co-ordinator for human rights (CM), who is responsible for the overall coordination of this aspect of foreign policy and for contacts with non-governmental organizations. Within the Directorate for International Organizations (DIO) the Division for Juridical and Social Affairs (DIO/JS) deals with humanitarian and juridical affairs, especially human rights in the organs of the United Nations and other global international organizations. The legal advisor and his staff (JURA), who are responsible for all legal affairs as they affect the entire Ministry, also deal with matters under the European Convention for Human Rights. EPC matters are handled by the coordinator for human rights under the responsibility of the director-general for political affairs (DGPZ). Human rights in particular countries are in the first instance handled

by the respective regional divisions. Certain specific themes
are dealt with by separate divisions within the Ministry.

A coordination committee deals with human rights affairs
(CCM). It consists of representatives of all policy units of
the ministry and meets once every three months. The coordinator for human rights and his deputy are the principal
officers responsible for coordinating the human rights
efforts of the ministry. There exists, however, no such institutional structure for coordinating human rights activities
as they affect other ministries. That means that below
cabinet level there is no systematic consideration of the role
of human rights *vis-à-vis* other non-foreign policy goals, although contacts exist with divisions within other ministries
relating to specific subjects. The appointment of the coordinator for human rights was the direct result of the parliamentary debate on the memorandum of 1979. Parliament
played a crucial role, especially at that time, in emphasizing
human rights factors as part of foreign policy. It still does
so, albeit in a less intensive manner. The individual views of
the person who occupies the post of Foreign Minister are
obviously of great importance as well.

NON-GOVERNMENTAL ORGANIZATIONS

Non-governmental organizations play an important role in
the formation of Dutch human rights policy. They deliver
commentary on that policy and provide suggestions and
proposals for strengthening human rights as part of foreign
policy. The papers and memoranda of the Minister of
Foreign Affairs are commented on. Their representatives
appear at hearings and approach officials of the Ministry
and members of parliament. The Ministry usually pays a
great deal of attention to the views of these organizations.
The Dutch delegation to the 1993 World Conference on
Human Rights in Vienna included two representatives of
non-governmental organizations.

Among the non-governmental organizations in this field
is the Dutch section of Amnesty International. This

important organization, which we have already mentioned in Chapter 5, has in the Netherlands now over 165,000 members, which is more than 1 per cent of the entire population – making it the largest national section in the world per head of population (with the possible exception of the Faeroe Islands). The question has often been raised as to why Amnesty is so strong in the Netherlands, much stronger than for example in neighbouring Belgium. The answer to that question is difficult to give. A possible explanation may be found in the fact that Dutch people traditionally feel concerned about developments abroad, both for economic and more idealistic reasons. In the past this was translated into foreign trade and colonialism as well as missionary work; nowadays it expresses itself again in foreign trade, in support of development cooperation and concern for human rights.[13]

Other important human rights organizations are the Netherlands Lawyers Committee for Human Rights (NJCM), and the Humanist Consultation for Human Rights studies (HOM). These and approximately ten similar organizations work together with organizations in the field of foreign policy, development cooperation, support for refugees, women's rights and religious organizations in the *Breed Mensenrechten Overleg* (BMO) ('Broad Human Rights Platform'). This is a loose form of cooperation which meets periodically. Its activities become more intensive at times, for instance during the debates over the 1979 Government Memorandum (for which it actually was founded) and in the preparation of the 1993 World Conference. The Netherlands Helsinki Committee focuses its attention on the observation of the 'human dimension' of the OSCE process by the states that adhere to the Helsinki Final Act and the conclusions of the follow-up meetings. The Netherlands Institute of Human Rights (SIM), a research institute of Utrecht University, collects information, studies the development of international human rights law and organizes conferences and seminars. The University of Limburg in Maastricht and Leiden University also have human rights research centres. Finally, PIOOM, *Projecten*

Interdisciplinair Onderzoek naar Oorzaken van Mensenrechten-schendigen ('Interdisciplinary Programme of Research on Root Causes of Human Rights Violations'), is an independent, non-partisan, non-profit organization located in Leiden which aims to promote and conduct research.

THE ADVISORY COMMITTEE ON HUMAN RIGHTS AND FOREIGN POLICY[14]

During the parliamentary debates that followed the publication of the 1979 Memorandum, it was agreed that the human rights efforts should be strengthened by the establishment of an official Advisory Committee. That committee was formally inaugurated by the Foreign Minister, Hans van den Broek, on 21 April 1983. Its task was to advise the minister 'on issues of human rights in relation to foreign policy upon request or on its own initiative'.[15] The Foreign Minister said in his inaugural address that the Committee should not deal solely with profound and demanding intellectual work. He continued:

> The Committee should direct its attention toward very *practical* aspects of foreign policy. This means that it should remain in touch with the overall direction of human rights policy. It means also that it must be aware of the administrative and political means and possibilities that are available. The Committee should for that reason be supplied with sufficient information. I will do my best to supply that necessary information.[16]

The Foreign Minister was well aware of the fact that the coming into being of the Advisory Committee had to a great extent been the result of intensive lobbying activities on the part of human rights organizations:

> The Committee is intended to give all sections of society that deal with human rights direct access to influence policy-making. Seen from the point of view of the Government, this is a dangerous operation. After all: no

Government Minister will be keen to facilitate direct criticism of his policies, especially on a subject like this. At the same time the Committee should be seen as a necessary step in making our democratic system more perfect and in promoting the openness of our governmental structure. That presupposes *faith*. *Faith* on the part of the Minister that the Committee will contribute in a positive and constructive way to the thinking of the policy-makers. *Faith* on the part of the Committee that something is *done* with its recommendations.[17]

From the beginning, therefore, the Committee had two kinds of parents who were at the same time the principal consumers of its reports: on the one hand, the Minister of Foreign Affairs and his staff, on the other hand the various non-governmental human rights organizations. Both parties viewed their common offspring, the Advisory Committee, and each other with considerable suspicion. For the Committee this meant careful manoeuvring so as to secure their common interest: a well-considered and effective human rights policy. The composition of the Committee helps to guarantee that the views of all parties are considered. It consists of a minimum of twelve and a maximum of seventeen members, independent experts who are nominated by the Minister of Foreign Affairs, and two advisory members from the Ministry who are selected by the Minister. The Committee's permanent secretary has his office in the Ministry, but is for his work accountable only to the Committee.

So far the Committee has published nineteen advisory reports[18] plus a number of shorter advisory letters. During the ten years of its existence it has not always been easy for the Committee to live up to the expectations of all parties involved. The Committee and the Ministry have, for instance, not always agreed on its choice of topics. Although the Committee is legally entitled to prepare advisory reports on its own initiative, in practice it would not be wise to choose only topics which the Minister has indicated he does not want. Its independent position may nevertheless require it to do so.

The Minister has issued written commentaries on most of the advisory reports, which sometimes have led to further oral communications. The Committee has acquired a position of its own by the quality of its reports and by serving as an intermediary between the Ministry and non-governmental organizations, with which it maintains close contacts. Its position of independence guarantees that it may see matters in a different light from the Minister and his officials. At the same time, it is sufficiently close to the Minister to ensure that its ideas and proposals will in fact reach him.

THE PRACTICE OF HUMAN RIGHTS POLICY

On the whole, Dutch human rights policy comes to the fore more in intergovernmental organizations, such as the United Nations, the European Union, the Council of Europe and the Organization on Security and Cooperation in Europe, than in bilateral relations. The intergovernmental organizations seem to offer a better forum and an opportunity to give expression to views on the subject of human rights.

Conflicts are not uncommon between foreign policy in the field of human rights and other sectors of public policy, especially international economic relations. An academic study of the making of Dutch foreign policy has looked at a number of such cases.[19] The study shows that the results of such conflicts more often will be in favour of the economic interests that are involved. The same group of researchers has also studied the *effect* of Dutch foreign policy.[20] Three of its chapters deal with human rights policy: human rights in Chile,[21] the UN convention against torture,[22] and European sanctions against South Africa.[23] In the first two cases, Dutch foreign policy had some measure of success; in the case of South Africa, only to a certain degree. In the case of Chile, the Netherlands made an important contribution to the condemnation mainly by the United Nations of the human rights violations in that country. The Netherlands – together with Sweden – played a leading role in the preparation and adoption of the UN Convention against Torture. It also had an important function in the acceptance of sanctions against South Africa by European Political Cooperation.

In his first follow-up memorandum to the original memorandum of 1979, the Minister of Foreign Affairs mentioned the leading role played by the Netherlands in the following subjects related to the development of human rights norms: the Convention on the Elimination of Discrimination against Women (1979), the Declaration on the Elimination of Intolerance and of Discrimination Based on Religion or Belief (1981), Principles of Medical Ethics (1982), the Convention against Torture (1984), and the Principles of International Adoption (1986).[24] A study of the Dutch policy role with regard to human rights issues in the United Nations has shown over the years an increasing activity and a relatively high measure of success.[25]

The Netherlands also played a leading role in the adoption of supervision mechanisms with regard to the 'human dimension' in the follow-up Conference in Vienna on Security and Cooperation in Europe (CSCE), which was adopted in 1989 (see Chapter 4, pp. 44–5). The Dutch proposal for a High Commissioner for National Minorities was adopted by the summit meeting of the CSCE participating states in Helsinki in July 1992. A Dutchman was the first person to be appointed to that position: former Foreign Minister Max van der Stoel.

At times, the Netherlands has used its foreign assistance programme to promote human rights. In 1982 it suspended the considerable aid programme to its former colony of Suriname in the wake of the killing of fifteen prominent opponents of the military regime. In 1987 civilian rule was restored, but no judicial investigation has ever taken place of the 1982 murders.[26] With the return of democratic government to Suriname the Netherlands has gradually resumed its aid programme.

The often rather outspoken attitude of the Netherlands government in relation to human rights is not universally appreciated. In 1991 it strongly criticized the role of the

military in Indonesia – another former colony – when it
opened fire on a peaceful demonstration in East Timor,
causing the death of of at least 100 people.[27] The
Netherlands, together with Denmark and Canada, briefly
suspended its aid programme to Indonesia. In 1992
Indonesia announced that henceforth it would no longer
accept development assistance from the Netherlands and
asked the Netherlands to terminate its chairmanship of the
Inter Governmental Group on Indonesia, the international
donor consortium which the Dutch government had
chaired since 1967. Indonesia referred to 'the reckless use
of development assistance as an instrument of intimidation
or as a tool for threatening Indonesia'.[28] Dutch–Indonesian
relations, which had always been delicate since the transfer
of sovereignty in 1949, have remained so ever since. Official
development assistance has stopped, though some aid is still
given through other, mainly non-governmental channels.
However, trade relations have increased.

CRITICISM

The foregoing points to a rather active Dutch human rights
policy. That does not mean, however, that the policy has remained beyond criticism. For instance, the Netherlands
Lawyers Committee for Human Rights has pleaded in a
report published in 1986 for more objectivity and transparency in Dutch human rights policy.[29] The report criticized the *ad hoc* manner in which measures were taken in
particular situations. It asked for a more structural approach based on precise criteria such as the following:

- point of departure should be that measures should
  have the character of remedy rather than of
  punishment;
- measures taken against a particular country should
  be in accordance with policy towards other countries
  where human rights violations are taking place (the
  principle of equal treatment);

- the local population should not be disproportionately victimized by such measures;
- if possible, measures should be taken jointly with other countries to obtain the greatest effect possible and to avoid unnecessary damage to bilateral relations.

The government has, however, never acted on these suggestions. It presumably prefers to deal with such questions on an *ad hoc* basis.

Non-government organizations have criticized the Dutch government among others for the following policy details:

- slow ratification procedures of international treaties;
- limited force in pushing human rights within the EPS framework;
- inadequate asylum and refugee policies;
- inadequate human rights policies in specific cases such as that of Turkey;
- too little attention paid to economic and social rights;
- too little attention paid to women's rights;
- a presumed lack of transparency of policy.

Clearly, it would be difficult for any government to satisfy fully the demands of non-governmental human rights organizations. Their comments and criticisms help to keep the Minister and his officials on their toes and to avoid smug self-satisfaction. Nevertheless, it would seem that, compared with other countries, the Netherlands has made a genuine effort to incorporate human rights in its foreign policy. Its relatively positive record domestically, as confirmed by the UN Human Rights Committee, helps to maintain its foreign policy standards. In 1988 the Dutch Foreign Minister proudly referred to a comment made by one of the experts serving on the UN Committee, who called the Netherlands 'the world laboratory of human rights'. That judgement may have been easy to reach, if one compares the record of the Netherlands with that of notorious human rights offenders at the time such as Uruguay, Peru or Romania.

The final judgement should be left to foreign observers. They may find some of the material presented in this chapter useful for reaching such a judgement. By way of provisional conclusion it may be suggested that the Netherlands has acquired a good international reputation both with regard to the care for human rights domestically and in its foreign policy. If not carefully maintained, such a reputation may, however, easily be lost again. That means that all concerned – that is the government, the Parliament, non-governmental organizations, the press and the general public – will have to work hard to maintain that reputation. As the French saying goes: *noblesse oblige*!

12 Concluding Observations

Everybody is in favour of human rights. That is true for governments that have made it a constituent element of their foreign policy. It is true for global and regional intergovernmental organizations that devote elegant words to it in international treaties and declarations. It is of course also true for non-governmental organizations that spend all or part of their efforts on it.

The Netherlands is in favour of human rights. So are the United States, Russia and even China. Amnesty International is in favour of human rights. In short, everybody is in favour; nobody is against. There appears to be 'consensus' – at least in words, if not always in deeds.

Such consensus has positive, but also less positive aspects. One of the positive aspects is that governments can be confronted with their own words – especially if actual practice is not fully in accordance with the theory. Such confrontations take place on a daily basis: in the UN Commission on Human Rights; in the framework of OSCE; and elsewhere. Sometimes this has effect and leads to an improvement of the human rights situation.

But consensus has also negative aspects. It can mean that one may close one's eyes to problems that are the consequences of greater respect for human rights; or to political dilemmas for which there are no simple solutions. Such dilemmas which have been discussed in the previous chapters are:

- the choice between human rights and non-intervention in domestic affairs;
- the choice between the right to national self-determination and territorial integrity;

165

- the choice between human rights and development assistance;
- the choice between human rights and *détente*.

Whoever decides to make human rights a constituent element of foreign policy will be confronted with such dilemmas. There are no simple recipes for solving them. Having weighed pros and cons, a decision must be taken. That is part and parcel of policy-making in general, including the making of foreign policy.

The greatest and most important problem remains the question of the universality of norms. Are human rights 'universal' or are they 'culturally relative'? There are no easy answers to that question, either. This book has been based on the idea of a gradually developing international agreement, while recognizing a certain degree of cultural diversity. That means the acceptance of the Universal Declaration of Human Rights as a 'common standard of achievement'.

Human rights are rights that are special and very important. They are now an essential part of international politics. They serve either as a goal or as an instrument of foreign policy. If seen as a goal, it means that one works for the improvement of human rights as such; seen as an instrument, it means that one uses human rights for other purposes, for example to strengthen national security. Both views have two aspects: on the one hand to contribute to international human rights standards, on the other, to apply those standards in cases of violations of human rights.

International human rights standards have been greatly developed since the Second World War. The Universal Declaration of Human Rights was followed by numerous treaties and declarations, globally as well as regionally, both with regard to human rights in general and specific rights in particular. Governments and political elites may by now be assumed to know what is permitted by these standards and what is not. This knowledge has, however, not yet reached all levels of society. This means that there is an important task for *human rights education*: the distribution of internationally accepted norms and values. For that purpose the translation of the most important texts into as many languages as possible is a *conditio sine qua non.*

The implementation of human rights standards has made less progress. International supervision mechanisms are insufficiently effective. This is not to say that no progress has been made at all. On a global level there are the organs of the United Nations and their rapporteurs and working groups. These have some effect, if only through the 'mobilization of shame'; governments do not like to be accused of human rights violations. Quite a few international human rights treaties contain reporting obligations. These are also of some importance, but the absence of effective sanctions for states that do not report or do not execute the recommendations of the supervisory organs, remains a major deficiency.

The most important supervisory mechanisms on a regional basis exist under the European Convention for the Protection of Human Rights and Fundamental Freedoms. As well as the West European states that founded the Council of Europe, more and more Central and East European states are acceding to the Convention. Perhaps in due course the successor states to the Soviet Union will also join. That emphasizes once more the urgent need to find solutions for the present overburdened system, which is in danger of declining under its own success. Supervision mechanisms in the other regions of the world are either less developed (Latin America, Africa) or entirely absent (Asia, the Pacific).

In the further development of supervision mechanisms consideration should be given to the fact that human rights violations occur increasingly by opposition groups not under government authority. Acts of terrorism, abductions, torture, and extra-judicial executions are human rights violations whether or not ordered by governments. Such groups often justify their activities by appealing to an aim of higher order: the fight against intolerable oppression or the liberation of their country. Governments may react by using means which are themselves violations of fundamental human rights. Violations of both kinds – by governments and non-governments alike – should be a subject of concern to those who work towards fundamental human rights in the world.

An important contribution to this work is made by non-governmental organizations. At the international level they contribute to the further development of international standards and they provide information to supervisory organs. In many fields there exists close cooperation between inter-governmental and non-governmental organizations. At the national level they observe critically the activities of the government and provide pertinent information to parliament and the press. In this area parliamentary and non-parliamentary groups can usefully complement each other.

The communication media are of vital importance in this area. Violations of human rights often occur in silence, behind the screens. Governments do not normally publish their human rights violations. The communication media distribute information, both about violations of human rights and about the reports of intergovernmental and non-governmental organizations, which are not widely read. Such reports, if further distributed by the press, radio and television, make such practices publicly known. Only if human rights violations are publicly known can 'world conscience' come into action. This world conscience or public opinion is in the final instance the most important weapon to be used against human rights violations. At the same time it is a highly uncertain and unreliable weapon. It is very difficult to say when and under what circumstances it will come into action. Fatigue symptoms and feelings of apathy among citizens, when they hear about ever-recurring human rights violations, can have a negative impact.

That is also true for a subject that so far has hardly been dealt with in this book: the concern for political refugees. There exists a clear relationship between the large and still increasing number of refugees in the world – estimates now range between 20 and 30 million – and human rights. The right to 'seek and enjoy asylum from persecution' which is contained in the Universal Declaration of Human Rights (article 14) is not part of internationally legally binding treaties. Nevertheless, it is a fact that most political refugees are the result of human rights violations elsewhere. It is therefore a matter of great concern that all over the world there is a decreasing willingness to accept refugees. It could well be possible that in the future the most important test of true concern for human rights might be a readiness to accept as many political refugees as possible.

Concern for human rights is permanent in nature. Nobody ever does enough on behalf of human rights. That is true for governments, for intergovernmental organizations, for national parliaments, for non-governmental organizations and for private individuals. It is praiseworthy if governments commit themselves to make human rights a central element of their foreign policy. They must, however, be continually reminded of that commitment.

Appendix

UNIVERSAL DECLARATION OF HUMAN RIGHTS

Adopted by the UN General Assembly Resolution 217 A
(III) of 10 December 1948

Preamble

Whereas recognition of the inherent dignity and of the
equal and inalienable rights of all members of the human
family is the foundation of freedom, justice and peace in
the world,

Whereas disregard and contempt for human rights have
resulted in barbarous acts which have outraged the conscience of mankind, and the advent of a world in which
human beings shall enjoy freedom of speech and belief and
freedom from fear and want has been proclaimed as the
highest aspiration of the common people,

Whereas it is essential, if man is not to be compelled to
have recourse, as a last resort, to rebellion against tyranny
and oppression, that human rights should be protected by
the rule of law,

Whereas it is essential to promote the development of
friendly relations between nations,

Whereas the peoples of the United Nations have in the
Charter reaffirmed their faith in fundamental human
rights, in the dignity and worth of the human person and in
the equal rights of men and women and have determined
to promote social progress and better standards of life in
larger freedom,

Whereas Member States have pledged themselves to
achieve, in cooperation with the United Nations, the promotion of universal respect for and observance of human
rights and fundamental freedoms,

Whereas a common understanding of these rights and freedoms is of the greatest importance for the full realization of this pledge,
Now, therefore,
The General Assembly,
Proclaims this Universal Declaration of Human Rights as a common standard of achievement for all peoples and all nations, to the end that every individual and every organ of society, keeping this Declaration constantly in mind, shall strive by teaching and education to promote respect for these rights and freedoms and by progressive measures, national and international, to secure their universal and effective recognition and observance, both among the peoples of Member States themselves and among the peoples of territories under their jurisdiction.

Article 1

All human beings are born free and equal in dignity and rights. They are endowed with reason and conscience and should act towards one another in a spirit of brotherhood.

Article 2

Everyone is entitled to all the rights and freedoms set forth in this Declaration, without distinction of any kind, such as race, colour, sex, language, religion, political or other opinion, national or social origin, property, birth or other status.
Furthermore, no distinction shall be made on the basis of the political, jurisdictional or international status of the country or territory to which a person belongs, whether it be independent, trust, non-self-governing or under any other limitation of sovereignty.

Article 3

Everyone has the right to life, liberty and security of person.

Article 4

No one shall be held in slavery or servitude; slavery and the slave trade shall be prohibited in all their forms.

Article 5

No one shall be subjected to torture or to cruel, inhuman or degrading treatment or punishment.

Article 6

Everyone has the right to recognition everywhere as a person before the law.

Article 7

All are equal before the law and are entitled without any discrimination to equal protection of the law. All are entitled to equal protection against any discrimination in violation of this Declaration and against any incitement to such discrimination.

Article 8

Everyone has the right to an effective remedy by the competent national tribunals for acts violating the fundamental rights granted him by the constitution or by law.

Article 9

No one shall be subjected to arbitrary arrest, detention or exile.

Article 10

Everyone is entitled in full equality to a fair and public hearing by an independent and impartial tribunal, in the determination of his rights and obligations and of any criminal charge against him.

Article 11

1. Everyone charged with a penal offence has the right to be presumed innocent until proved guilty according to law in a public trial at which he has had all the guarantees necessary for his defence.

2. No one shall be held guilty of any penal offence on account of any act or omission which did not constitute a penal offence, under national or international law, at the time when it was committed. Nor shall a heavier penalty be imposed than the one that was applicable at the time the penal offence was committed.

Article 12

No one shall be subjected to arbitrary interference with his privacy, family, home or correspondence, nor to attacks upon his honour and reputation. Everyone has the right to the protection of the law against such interference or attacks.

Article 13

1. Everyone has the right to freedom of movement and residence within the borders of each State.

2. Everyone has the right to leave any country, including his own, and to return to his country.

Article 14

1. Everyone has the right to seek and to enjoy in other countries asylum from persecution.

2. This right may not be invoked in the case of prosecutions genuinely arising from non-political crimes or from acts contrary to the purposes and principles of the United Nations.

Article 15

1. Everyone has the right to a nationality.
2. No one shall be arbitrarily deprived of his nationality nor denied the right to change his nationality.

Article 16

1. Men and women of full age, without any limitations due to race, nationality or religion, have the right to marry and to found a family. They are entitled to equal rights as to marriage, during marriage and at its dissolution.
2. Marriage shall be entered into only with the free and full consent of the intending spouses.
3. The family is the natural and fundamental group of society and is entitled to protection by society and the State.

Article 17

1. Everyone has the right to own property alone as well as in association with others.
2. No one shall be arbitrarily deprived of his property.

Article 18

Everyone has the right to freedom of thought, conscience and religion; this right includes freedom to change his religion or belief, and freedom, either alone or in community with others and in public or private, to manifest his religion or belief in teaching, practice, worship and observance.

Article 19

Everyone has the right to freedom of opinion and expression; this right includes freedom to hold opinions without interference and to seek, receive and impart information and ideas through any media and regardless of frontiers.

Article 20

1. Everyone has the right to freedom of peaceful assembly and association.

2. No one may be compelled to belong to an association.

Article 21

1. Everyone has the right to take part in the government of his country, directly or through freely chosen representatives.

2. Everyone has the right to equal access to public service in his country.

3. The will of the people shall be the basis of the authority of government; this will shall be expressed in periodic and genuine elections which shall be by universal suffrage and shall be held by secret vote or by equivalent free voting procedures.

Article 22

Everyone, as a member of society, has the right to social security and is entitled to realization, through national effort and international co-operation and in accordance with the organization and resources of each State, of the economic, social and cultural rights indispensable for his dignity and the free development of his personality.

Article 23

1. Everyone has the right to work, to free choice of employment, to just and favourable conditions of work and to protection against unemployment.

2. Everyone, without any discrimination, has the right to equal pay for equal work.

3. Everyone who works has the right to just and favourable remuneration ensuring for himself and his family an existence worthy of human dignity, and supplemented, if necessary, by other means of social protection.

4. Everyone has the right to form and to join trade unions for the protection of his interests.

Article 24

Everyone has the right to rest and leisure, including reasonable limitation of working hours and periodic holidays with pay.

Article 25

1. Everyone has the right to a standard of living adequate for the health and well-being of himself and of his family, including food, clothing, housing and medical care and necessary social services, and the right to security in the event of unemployment, sickness, disability, widowhood, old age or other lack of livelihood in circumstances beyond his control.

2. Motherhood and childhood are entitled to special care and assistance. All children, whether born in or out of wedlock, shall enjoy the same social protection.

Article 26

1. Everyone has the right to education. Education shall be free, at least in the elementary and fundamental stages. Elementary education shall be compulsory. Technical and professional education shall be made generally available and higher education shall be equally accessible to all on the basis of merit.

2. Education shall be directed to the full development of the human personality and to the strengthening of respect for human rights and fundamental freedoms. It shall promote understanding, tolerance and friendship among all nations, racial or religious groups, and shall further the activities of the United Nations for the maintenance of peace.

3. Parents have a prior right to choose the kind of education that shall be given to their children.

Article 27

1. Everyone has the right freely to participate in the cultural life of his community, to enjoy the arts and to share in scientific advancement and its benefits.

2. Everyone has the right to the protection of the moral and material interests resulting from any scientific, literary or artistic production of which he is the author.

Article 28

Everyone is entitled to a social and international order in which the rights and freedoms set forth in this Declaration can be fully realized.

Article 29

1. Everyone has duties to the community in which alone the free and full development of his personality is possible.

2. In the exercise of his rights and freedoms, everyone shall be subject only to such limitations as are determined by law solely for the purpose of securing due recognition and respect for the rights and freedoms of others and of meeting the just requirements of morality, public order and the general welfare in a democratic society.

3. These rights and freedoms may in no case be exercised contrary to the purposes and principles of the United Nations.

Article 30

Nothing in this Declaration may be interpreted as implying for any State, group or person any right to engage in any activity or to perform any act aimed at the destruction of any of the rights and freedoms set forth herein.

Notes and References

Chapter 1 Introduction

1. Ministry of Foreign Affairs of the Kingdom of the Netherlands, *Human Rights and Foreign Policy*, memorandum presented to the Lower House of the States General of the Kingdom of the Netherlands on 3 May 1979 by the Minister for Foreign Affairs and the Minister for Development Cooperation, (English version), p. 15.
2. Michael Ross Fowler, *Thinking about Human Rights: Contending Approaches to Human Rights in U.S. Foreign Policy*, Lanham: University Press of America, 1987, p. 70.
3. Maurice Cranston, *What are Human Rights?*, New York: Taplinger, 1973, p. 70.
4. Hedley Bull, 'Human Rights and World Politics', in Ralph Pettman (ed.), *Moral Claims in World Affairs*, London: Croom Helm, 1979, p. 79.
5. *Human Rights and Foreign Policy* (see note 1 above), p. 16.
6. For the texts of these documents, see, for instance, Walter Laqueur and Barry Rubin (eds), *The Human Rights Reader*, New York: New American Library, rev. edn, 1989, pp. 59 ff.
7. See further, Farokh Jhabala, 'On Human Rights and the Socio-Economic Context', *Netherlands International Law Review*, XXXI (1984), p. 164.
8. See Cees Flinterman, 'Three Generations of Human Rights', in Jan Berting *et al.* (eds), *Human Rights in a Pluralist World: Individuals and Collectivities*, Westport and London: Meckler, 1990, pp. 75–82.
9. Katarina Tomasevksi, 'The Right to Peace', in Richard Pierre Claude and Burns H. Weston (eds), *Human Rights in the World Community: Issues and Actions*,

Philadelphia: University of Pennsylvania Press, 1989, p. 168. Reprinted from *Current Research on Peace and Violence*, vol. 5, no. 1 (1982), pp. 42–69.

10. See 'The Syracusa Principles on the Limitations and Derogation Provisions in the International Covenant on Civil and Political Rights', *Human Rights Quarterly*, vol. 7, no. 1 (February 1985), pp. 3 ff.
11. See Philip Alston, 'Conjuring Up New Human Rights: A Proposal for Quality Control', *American Journal of International Law*, vol. 78, no. 3 (1984), pp. 607–21.
12. *Human Rights and Foreign Policy* (note 1 above), p. 16.

Chapter 2 Universality and Cultural Relativism

1. See Philip Alston, 'The Universal Declaration at 35: Western and Passé or Alive and Universal?', *The Review of the International Commission of Jurists*, no. 31 (December 1983), pp. 60–70.
2. Cf. Adamantia Pollis and Peter Schwab, 'Human Rights: A Western Construct with Limited Applicability', in Pollis and Schwab (eds), *Human Rights: Cultural and Ideological Perspectives*, New York: Praeger, 1980, p. 14. See also C. Tomuschat, 'Is Universality of Human Rights Standards an Outdated and Utopian Concept?', in E. Bieber (ed.), *Das Europa der Zweiten Generation*, Munich: Engel Verlag, 1981.
3. See R. Panikkar, 'Is the Notion of Human Rights a Western Concept?', *Diogenes*, 120 (1985), p. 75.
4. A useful survey of the literature is contained in Alison Dundes Renteln, *International Human Rights: Universalism Versus Relativism*, Newbury Park: Sage, 1990.
5. See Fernando R. Tesón, 'International Human Rights and Cultural Relativism', *Virginia Journal of International Law*, vol. 25, no. 4 (1985), p. 870.
6. See R.J. Vincent, *Human Rights and International Relations*, Cambridge: Cambridge University Press, 1986, p. 37.
7. Rhoda E. Howard, *Human Rights in Commonwealth Africa*, Totowa, N.J.: Rowman & Littlefield, 1986, p. 17.

Howard later reiterated her criticism of the notion of cultural relativism: see Rhoda E. Howard, 'Cultural Absolutism and the Nostalgia for Community', *Human Rights Quarterly*, vol. 15, no. 2 (May 1993), pp. 315–38.

8.   Jack Donnelly, *Universal Human Rights in Theory and Practice*, Ithaca, N.Y.: Cornell University Press, 1989, p. 110.

9.   Donnelly, *Universal Human Rights* (note 8 above), p. 57.

10. Cf. Ann Elizabeth Mayer, 'Current Muslim Thinking on Human Rights', in Abdullahi Ahmed an-Na'im and Francis M. Deng (eds), *Human Rights in Africa: Cross-Cultural Perspectives*, Washington D.C.: The Brookings Institution, 1990, p. 154.

11. UN General Assembly, *Official Records*, 183rd plenary meeting, 10 December 1948.

12. Cf. Antonio Cassese, *Human Rights in a Changing World*, Cambridge: Polity Press, 1990, p. 37.

13. United Nations General Assembly, A/CONF.157/23, 12 July 1993, *Vienna Declaration and Programme of Action*.

14. Thomas Buergenthal, *International Human Rights in a Nutshell*, St. Paul, Minn.: West Publishing Co., 1988, p. 32.

15. Cf. J.H. Burgers and H. Danelius, *The United Nations Convention against Torture*, Dordrecht: Martinus Nijhoff Publishers, 1988.

16. Adnan Buyung Nasution, *The Aspiration for Constitutional Government in Indonesia: A Socio-Legal Study of the Indonesian Konstituante 1956–1959*, doctoral dissertation Utrecht University, 1992, p. 407.

17. See Statement by Mr Ali Alatas, Minister for Foreign Affairs of the Republic of Indonesia, before the Second World Conference on Human Rights, Vienna, 14 June 1993.

18. Vincent, *Human Rights* (note 6 above) p. 105.

Chapter 3 Policy Choices

1.   Ministry of Foreign Affairs of the Kingdom of the Netherlands, *Human Rights and Foreign Policy*,

Memorandum presented to the Lower House of the States General of the Kingdom of the Netherlands on 3 May 1979 by the Minister for Foreign Affairs and the Minister for Development Co-operation (English version), p. 136.

2. Max van der Stoel, 'De Rechten van de Mens in de Oost-West betrekkingen', ('Human Rights in East–West Relations'), in Ph. P. Everts and J.L. Heldring (eds), *Netherland en de Rechten van de Mens*, Baarn: Anthos, 1981, p. 79; translated from the original Dutch.

3. See Amnesty International, *Turkey: A Policy of Denial – Update 1*, AI index: EUR 44/24/95, February 1995; *Turkey: Mothers of 'Disappeared' Take Action'*, AI index: EUR 44/55/95, May 1995.

4. See Leo Zwaak, 'A Friendly Settlement in the European Inter-State Complaints Against Turkey', *SIM Newsletter*, no. 13, February 1986, pp. 44–8.

5. Only at a very late stage has the German government expressed criticism of the Turkish treatment of the Kurds.

Chapter 4 Policy Instruments

1. E. Luard, *Human Rights and Foreign Policy*, Oxford: Pergamon Press, 1981, pp. 26–7.

2. It is to be distinguished from 'parliamentary diplomacy' or 'conference diplomacy', which applies mainly to multilateral fora. Cf. Johan Kaufmann, *Conference Diplomacy: An Introductory Analysis*, Dordrecht: Martinus Nijhoff, 2nd revised edn, 1988.

3. Article J.1 of the Maastricht treaty on European Union states that the Union and its members shall define and implement a common foreign and security policy.

4. Cf. Leo Zwaak, 'A Friendly Settlement in the European Inter-State Complaints against Turkey', *SIM Newsletter*, no. 13, February 1986, pp. 44–8. This view was confirmed in December 1992, when the European Committee for the Prevention of Torture issued a public statement which concluded that the practice of

torture and other forms of severe ill-treatment of persons in police custody still remained widespread in Turkey. See European Committee for the Prevention of Torture and Inhuman or Degrading Treatment or Punishment, *Public Statement on Turkey*, adopted on 15 December 1992.

5. Cf. Dutch Human Rights and Foreign Policy Advisory Committee, *Development Cooperation and Human Rights*, The Hague: Ministry of Foreign Affairs, 1987, pp. 32–4.

6. Luard, *Human Rights*, (note 1 above) pp. 28–9.

7. UNGA Resolution 2625 (XXV).

8. Cf. Peter Malanczuk, *Humanitarian Intervention and the Legitimacy of the Use of Force*, Amsterdam: Het Spinhuis, 1993; Adam Roberts, 'Humanitarian War: Military Intervention and Human Rights', *International Affairs*, vol. 69, no. 3, pp. 429–50; Nigel Rodley (ed.), *To Loose the Bands of Wickedness: International Intervention in Defence of Human Rights*, London: Brassey's, 1992.

9. Cf. Peter Malanczuk, 'The Kurdish Crisis and Allied Intervention in the Aftermath of the Second Gulf War', *European Journal of International Law*, vol. 2 (1991), pp. 114–32.

10. S/RES/688 (1991).

11. S/RES/733 (1992).

12. Michael Akehurst, 'Humanitarian Intervention', in Hedley Bull, *Intervention in World Politics*, Oxford: Clarendon Press, 1985, pp. 97–9.

13. Cf. Arie Bloed and Pieter van Dijk, 'Human Rights and Non-Intervention', in A. Bloed and P. van Dijk (eds), *Essays on Human Rights in the Helsinki Process*, Dordrecht: Martinus Nijhoff, 1985, pp. 61 ff.

14. R.J. Vincent, *Non-Intervention and International Order*, Princeton N.J.: Princeton University Press, 1974, p. 346.

15. Cf. Marc Bossuyt, 'Human Rights and Non-intervention in Domestic Matters', *ICJ Review*, 35 (December 1985), pp. 50–1.

16. R.J. Vincent, *Human Rights and International Relations*, Cambridge: Cambridge University Press, 1986, p. 66.

17. See Arie Bloed, 'The Human Dimension of the OSCE: More Words than Deeds?' *Helsinki Monitor*, vol. 6, no. 4 (1995), pp. 23–9.

18. Luard, *Human Rights* (note 1 above), p. 8.

19. David Owen, *Human Rights*, London: Jonathan Cape, 1978, p. 2. See also Abraham M. Sirkin, 'Can a Human Rights Policy be Consistent?', in Peter G. Brown and Douglas MacLean (eds), *Human Rights and U.S. Foreign Policy*, Lexington Mass.: Lexington Books, 1979, pp. 199–213.

Chapter 5 Domestic Sources of Foreign Policy

1. See Donald M. Fraser, 'Congress's Role in the Making of International Human Rights Policy', in Donald P. Kommers and Gilburt D. Loescher (eds.), *Human Rights and American Foreign Policy*, Notre Dame and London: University of Notre Dame Press, 1979, p. 248.

2. *Human Rights in Developing Countries 1986: A Yearbook on Countries Receiving Norwegian Aid*, Oslo: Norweigian University Press, 1986.

3. *Human Rights in Developing Countries 1987/1988*, Copenhagen: Akademisk Forlag, 1988.

4. Manfred Nowak and Theresa Swinehart (eds), *Human Rights in Developing Countries 1989 Yearbook*, Kehl, Strasbourg, Arlington: N.P. Engel, 1989; Bård-Anders Andreassen and Theresa Swinehart (eds), *Human Rights in Developing Countries 1990 Yearbook*, Kehl, Strasbourg, Arlington: N.P. Engel, 1991; Bård-Anders Andreassen and Theresa Swinehart (eds), *Human Rights in Developing Countries 1991 Yearbook*, Oslo: Norwegian University Press, 1992; Bård-Anders Andreassen and Theresa Swinehart (eds), *Human Rights in Developing Countries 1993 Yearbook*, Oslo: Nordic Human Rights Publications, 1993; Peter Baehr, Hilde Hey, Jacqueline Smith and Theresa Swinehart (eds), *Human Rights in Developing Countries 1994 Yearbook and 1995 Yearbook*, Deventer: Kluwer Law and

Taxation, 1994; The Hague/Boston/London: Kluwer Law International, 1995.

5. See Laurie Wiseberg and Harry Scoble, 'Monitoring Human Rights Violations: The Role of Nongovernmental Organizations', in Donald P. Kommers and Gilburt D. Loescher (eds), *Human Rights and American Foreign Policy*, Notre Dame and London: University of Notre Dame Press, 1979, pp. 179–208; Henry J. Steiner, *Diverse Partners: Non-Governmental Organizations in the Human Rights Movement*, Cambridge, Mass.: Harvard Law School Human Rights Program, 1991; *The Role of Non-Governmental Organizations in the Promotion and Protection of Human Rights*, Leiden: NJCM Boekerij, 1991.

6. *Statute of Amnesty International*, as amended by the 22nd International Council Meeting, Ljubljana, Slovenia, 12–20 August 1995. See also Peter R. Baehr, 'Amnesty International and its Self-Imposed Limited, Mandate', *Netherlands Quarterly of Human Rights*, Vol. 12, no. 1 (1994), pp. 5–21.

7. Amnesty International, *International Report 1995*, London, 1995.

8. Peter R. Baehr, 'The General Assembly: Negotiating the Convention on Torture', in David P. Forsythe (ed.), *The United Nations in the World Political Economy: Essays in Honour of Leon Gordenker*, London: Macmillan, 1989, p. 47.

Chapter 6 Intergovernmental Organizations

1. Parts of this chapter have been published before, in Peter R. Baehr and Leon Gordenker, *The United Nations in the 1990s*, London: Macmillan, 2nd edn, 1994.

2. The Commission may also meet exceptionally – between regular sessions – if a majority of members so decides. This happened twice in 1992, when the Commission met to discuss the human rights situation in the former Yugoslavia. In May 1994, the Commission held a special session on the situation in Rwanda.

3. A major study on the work of the Commission is Howard Tolley Jr., *The UN Commission on Human Rights*, Boulder and London: Westview Press, 1987. See also Philip Alston, 'The Commission on Human Rights', in Philip Alston (ed.), *The United Nations and Human Rights: A Critical Appraisal*, Oxford: Clarendon Press, 1992, pp. 126–210.

4. Variously, the terms 'special rapporteur' and 'special representative' are used. See Alston, *The United Nations*, (note 3 above), p. 160.

5. 'The UN Commission on Human Rights and the new Working Group on Arbitrary Detention', *ICJ Review*, no. 46 (June 1991), pp. 23–32.

6. For relevant material, see 'Interview with Prof. Kooijmans, Special Rapporteur on Torture for the United Nations' Commission on Human Rights', *SIM Newsletter*, no. 16 (November 1986), pp. 3–13; 'Interview with Max van der Stoel, Special Rapporteur of the UN Commission on Human Rights on Iraq', *Netherlands Quarterly of Human Rights*, vol. 10, no. 3 (1992), pp. 277–82; 'Interview with Special Rapporteur on Torture, Nigel Rodley', *Netherlands Quarterly of Human Rights*, vol. 13, no. 4 (1995), pp. 435–9.

7. Cf. Jack Donnelly, 'Human Rights at the United Nations 1955–1985: The Question of Bias', *International Studies Quarterly* vol. 32 (1988), pp. 275–303.

8. See D. McGoldrick, *The Human Rights Committee: Its Role in the Development of the International Convenant on Civil and Political Rights*, Oxford: Clarendon Press, 1991; Torkel Opsahl, 'The Human Rights Committee', in Alston, *The United Nations* (note 3 above), pp. 369–443; Ineke Boerefijn, 'Towards a System of Supervision. The Human Rights Committee's Role in Reforming the Reporting Procedure under Article 40 of the Covenant on Civil and Political Rights', *Human Rights Quarterly*, vol. 17, no. 4 (1995), pp. 766–93.

9. For more details, see Lammy Betten, 'The International Implementation of Economic and Social Rights by ILO', *Newsletter SIM Netherlands Quarterly of Human Rights*, vol. 6, no. 2 (1988), pp. 29–42.

10. John Humphrey, *No Distant Millenium: The International Law of Human Rights*, Paris: UNESCO, 1989, p. 130.
11. See P. van Dijk and G.J.H. van Hoof, *Theory and Practice of the European Convention on Human Rights*, Deventer: Kluwer, 1990.
12. See Leo Zwaak, 'A Friendly Settlement in the European Inter-State Complaints Against Turkey', *SIM Newsletter*, no. 13 (February 1986), pp. 44–8.
13. 'Protocol No. 11 to the Convention for the Protection of Human Rights and Fundamental Freedoms, Restructuring the Control Machinery established thereby', *Netherlands Quarterly of Human Rights*, vol. 12, no. 2 (1994), pp. 227–37. See also K. de Vey Mestdagh, 'Reform of the European Convention on Human Rights in a Changing Europe', in Rick Lawson and Matthijs de Blois (eds), The Dynamics of the Protection of Human Rights in Europe, Dordrecht/Boston/London: Martinus Nijhoff, 1994, pp. 337–60.
14. See Cecilia Medina Quiroga, *The Battle of Human Rights: Gross, Systematic Violations and the Inter-American System*, Dordrecht: Martinus Nijhoff, 1988; Cecilia Medina Quiroga, 'The Right of Individual Complaint before the Inter-American Commission on Human Rights: Some Problems of Law and Practice'; Claudio Grossman, 'Democracy, Human Rights and Non-Intervention in the organization of American states', and Tom Farer, 'The Inter-American Human Rights Enforcement System: A Critique', Training Course on International Human Rights Law for Judges and Lawyers of South America, SIM Special, No. 13, pp. 158–201.
15. Christina M. Cerna, 'US Death Penalty Tested Before the Inter-American Commission on Human Rights', *Netherlands Quarterly of Human Rights*, vol. 10, no. 2 (1992), pp. 155–65. More generally see David Forsythe, 'Human Rights, the United States and the Organization of American States', *Human Rights Quarterly*, vol. 13, no. 1 (February 1991), pp. 66–98.
16. For the results of interviews with current and former judges of the Court, see Lynda E. Frost, 'The Evolution

of the Inter-American Court of Human Rights: Reflections of Present and Former Judges', *Human Rights Quarterly*, vol. 14, no. 2 (May 1992), pp. 171–205.

17. Cecilia Medina, 'The Inter-American System', *Netherlands Quarterly of Human Rights*, vol. 13, no. 1 (1995), p. 79.

18. Claude E. Welch Jr., 'The African Commission on Human and Peoples' Rights: A Five Year Report and Assessment', *Human Rights Quarterly*, vol. 14, no. 1 (February 1992), pp. 44 and 49.

19. Cf. Welch, *The African Commission* (note 18 above), p. 55, citing Wolfgang Benedek, 'The 9th Session of the African Commission on Human and Peoples' Rights', *Human Rights Law Journal*, vol. 12, no. 5 (May 1991), p. 217.

20. Cf. Welch, *The African Commission* (note 18 above), p. 54; Felice D. Gaer, 'First Fruits: Reporting by States under the African Charter on Human and Peoples' Rights', *Netherlands Quarterly of Human Rights*, vol. 10, no. 1 (1992), pp. 29–42; Philip Vuciri Ramaga, 'The Tenth Session of the African Commission on Human and Peoples' Rights', *Netherlands Quarterly of Human Rights*, vol. 10, no. 3 (1992), p. 362.

21. Anselm Chidi Odinkalu, 'Proposals for the Review of the Rules of Procedure of the African Commission on Human and Peoples' Rights', *Human Rights Quarterly*, vol. 15, no. 3 (1993), pp. 533–48; Wolfgang Benedek, 'Enforcement of Human and Peoples' Rights in Africa: The Communication System and State Reporting under the African Charter', in Jacqueline Smith and Leo Zwaak (eds), *International Protection of Human Rights, SIM Special*, no. 15, Utrecht, 1995, pp. 23–43.

Chapter 7 The United States

1. Cf. M. Glen Johnson, 'The Contributions of Eleanor and Franklin Roosevelt to the Development of International Protection for Human Rights', *Human Rights Quarterly*, vol. 9, no. 1 (February 1987), pp. 19–48.

2. Lloyd Jensen, *Explaining Foreign Policy*, Englewood Cliffs N.J.:Prentice Hall, 1982, p. 84.
3. Paula Dobriansky, 'U.S. Human Rights Policy: An Overview', *Department of State Bulletin*, October 1988, p. 54.
4. Cf. his 'Morality and Foreign Policy', *Foreign Affairs* 1985, pp. 205–18.
5. As cited by Roberta Cohen, 'Human Rights Decision-Making in the Executive Branch: Some Proposals for a Coordinated Strategy', in Donald P. Kommers and Gilburt D. Loescher (eds), *Human Rights and American Foreign Policy*, Notre Dame and London: Notre Dame University Press, 1979, p. 217.
6. See Stanley Hoffmann, *Primacy or World Order: American Foreign Policy since the Cold War*, New York: McGraw-Hill, 1978; and *Duties Beyond Borders: On the Limits and Possibilities of Ethical International Politics*, Syracuse: Syracuse University Press, 1981.
7. See Joshua Muravchik, *The Uncertain Crusade: Jimmy Carter and the Dilemmas of Human Rights Policy*, Lanham, Md.: Hamilton Press, 1986.
8. See Tamar Jacoby, 'The Reagan Turnaround on Human Rights', *Foreign Affairs*, 64 (Summer 1986), pp. 1066–86. For a comparison of the human rights policies of the Carter and Reagan Administrations, see David P. Forsythe, 'Human Rights in U.S. Foreign Policy: Retorspect and Prospect', *Political Science Quarterly*, vol. 105, no. 1 (1990), p. 447.
9. Cf. Forsythe, 'Human Rights' (note 8 above), p. 451: 'Indeed, in the final years of the second Reagan administration, any number of staunch anticommunists discovered that an active and even-handed attention to human rights *contributed* to the containment of the Soviet Union.'
10. Jeane Kirkpatrick, 'Dictatorships and Double Standards', *Commentary*, November 1979, pp. 29–40.
11. Cyrus R. Vance, 'The Human Rights Imperative', *Foreign Policy*, 6 (1986), p. 9.

12. See J.J. Shestack and R. Cohen, 'International Human Rights: A Role for the United States', *Virginia Journal of International Law*, 14 (Summer 1974), pp. 673–701.

13. Mark L. Schneider, 'A New Administration's New Policy: The Rise to Power of Human Rights', in Peter G. Brown and Douglas MacLean (eds), *Human Rights and U.S. Foreign Policy: Principles and Applications*, Lexington, Mass. and Toronto: Lexington Books, 1979, pp. 3–13.

14. As quoted in Tom Harkin, 'Human Rights and Foreign Aid: Forging an Unbreakable Link', in Brown and MacLean, *Human Rights* (note 13 above), p. 17.

15. C.W. Tarr, 'Human Rights and Arms Transfer Policy', in V. Nanda, J. Scarritt and G. Shepherd (eds), *Global Human Rights: Public Policies, Comparative Measures and NGO Strategies*, Boulder, Col.: Westview Press, 1981, p. 61.

16. For a survey of legislation adopted by the US Congress relating to human rights and foreign policy, see David P. Forsythe, *Human Rights and U.S. Foreign Policy: Congress Reconsidered*, Gainesville: University of Florida Press, 1988, pp. 1–23.

17. Dobriansky, 'U.S. Human Rights Policy' (note 3 above), p. 55. However, at the UN World Conference on Human Rights, held in June 1993 in Vienna, Secretary of State Warren Christopher said, after having announced that the Clinton administration was planning to obtain the consent of the Senate to ratify the International Convention on the Elimination of All Forms of Racial Discrimination: 'We strongly support the general goals of the other treaties that we have signed but not yet ratified. The Convention on the Elimination of all Forms of Discrimination against Women; The American Convention on Human Rights; *and the International Covenant on Economic, Social and Cultural Rights* [italics added]: All of these will constitute important advances, and our Administration will turn to them as soon as the Senate has acted on the racism Convention.' *US Department of State Dispatch*, vol. 4, no. 25.

18. See Judith de Neufville, 'Human Rights Reporting as a Policy Tool: An Examination of the State Department Country Reports', *Human Rights Quarterly*, vol. 8, no. 4 (November 1986), pp. 681–99; Edward S. Maynard, 'The Bureaucracy and Implementation of U.S. Human Rights Policy', *Human Rights Quarterly*, vol. 11, no. 2 (May 1989), p. 229.

19. Lawyers Committee for Human Rights, *Human Rights and U.S. Foreign Policy*, New York, 1992, p. 8.

20. Inaugural address of President Jimmy Carter, in *Public Papers of the Presidents of the United States 1977*, Book 1, Washington D.C.: US Government Printing Office, 1977, pp. 2–3.

21. Speech at the University of Notre Dame, 22 May 1977.

22. Michael Stohl, David Carlton, Mark Gibney and Geoffrey Martin, 'US Foreign Policy, Human Rights and Multilateral Assistance', in David P. Forsythe (ed.), *Human Rights and Development: International Views*, London: Macmillan, 1989, p. 207.

23. US Department of State, *Country Report on Human Rights Practices for 1981*, February 1982, p. 11.

24. Cohen, 'Human Rights Decision-Making' (note 5 above), p. 218.

25. Cited by Cohen, 'Human Rights Decision-Making' (note 5 above), p. 221.

26. See Maynard, 'The Bureaucracy' (note 18 above), pp. 175–248.

27. Cf. Maynard, *ibid*, pp. 205–12.

28. Forsythe, *Human Rights* (note 16 above), p. 121.

29. Cf. Maynard, 'The Bureaucracy' (note 18 above), p. 191: 'After eleven years, HA [the Bureau of Human Rights and Humanitarian Affairs] appears to have become institutionalized in State Department decision-making.'

30. Cf. Forsythe, 'Human Rights' (note 8 above), p. 442.

31. Maynard, 'The Bureaucracy' (note 18 above), p. 212.

32. For a full treatment, see Richard B. Lillich, *U.S. Ratification of the Human Rights Treaties*, Charlottesville, Va.: University Press of Virginia, 1981; Natalie Hevener

Kaufman, *Human Rights Treaties and the Senate: A History of Opposition*, Chapel Hill and London: The University of North Carolina Press, 1990.

33. *Congressional Record – Senate*, 2 April 1992, p. S 4783–4784. Cf. Louis Henkin, 'US Ratification of Human Rights Conventions: The Ghost of Senator Bricker', *American Journal of International Law*, vol. 89 (1995), pp. 341–50.
34. Cf. Lawrence J. LeBlanc, *The United States and the Genocide Convention*, Durham and London: Duke University Press, 1991, p. 144.
35. Cf. note 17 above.
36. D. Carleton and M. Stohl, 'The Foreign Policy of Human Rights: Rhetoric and Reality from Jimmy Carter to Ronald Reagan', *Human Rights Quarterly*, vol. 7, no. 2 (May 1985), pp. 205–29.
37. Carleton and Stohl, *ibid*, p. 214.
38. US Department of State, *Country Reports on Human Rights Practices for 1988*, 101st Congress, 1st Session, S. Prt. 101–3, Washington D.C.: Government Printing Office, 1989, pp. 1366–87.
39. *Human Rights and U.S. Foreign Policy* (note 19 above).
40. *NRC Handelsblad* (Rotterdam), 8 January 1983; translated from the original Dutch.
41. Stohl *et al.*, 'U.S. Foreign Policy' (note 22 above), p. 209.
42. Cf. Maynard, 'The Bureaucracy' (note 18 above), p. 192.

Chapter 8 The Soviet Union and Its Successors

1. Winston S. Churchill, *The Gathering Storm*, London: Cassell & Co., 1948, p. 403.
2. Vernon V. Aspaturian, *Process and Power in Soviet Foreign Policy*, Boston: Little, Brown, 1971; Harry Gelman, 'Gorbachev's Dilemmas and his Conflicting Foreign Policy Goals', *Orbis* (Summer 1986), pp. 231–47; Dimitri K. Simes, 'Gorbachev: A New Foreign Policy?', *Foreign Affairs*, vol. 65, no. 3 (1986), pp. 477–500; Jef Checkel, 'Ideas, Institutions, and the Gorbachev

Foreign Policy Revolution', *World Politics,* vol. 45, no. 2 (Jan. 1993), pp. 271–300.

3. Alvin Z. Rubinstein, 'Sources of Soviet Policy', in Rubinstein (ed.), *Soviet Foreign Policy since World War II,* Boston: Little, Brown & Co., 2nd edn, 1971, p. 330.

4. Aspaturian, *Process and Power* (note 2 above), p. 330.

5. W.M. Chvostov, 'Bilanz eines halben Jahrhunderts sowjetischer Aussenpolitik' ('Balance Sheet of Half a Century of Soviet Foreign Policy'), in *50 Jahre Leninische Aussenpolitik* ('Fifty Years of Leninist Foreign Policy'), *Deutsche Aussenpolitik,* Sonderheft 1 (1968), pp. 29–30.

6. See Rubinstein, 'Sources of Soviet Policy' (note 3 above), p. 318 ff.; also E. Poppe, 'Human Rights and Peaceful Coexistence', *Bulletin GDR Committee for Human Rights,* vol. 14, no. 3 (1988), pp. 172–82.

7. Arie Bloed and Fried van Hoof, 'Some Aspects of the Socialist View of Human Rights', in A. Bloed and P. van Dijk (eds), *Essays on Human Rights in the Helsinki Process,* Dordrecht: Nijhoff, 1985, pp. 34–5.

8. United Nations General Assembly, *Official Records,* 183rd plenary meeting, 10 December 1948, p. 929.

9. V. Chkhikvadze, 'Interstate Cooperation on Human Rights', *International Affairs (Moscow),* 11 (1985), p. 32.

10. See N. Graf, 'Indivisibility of Human Rights – A New Start', *Bulletin of the GDR Committee for Human Rights,* no. 1/1986, p. 16; E. Poppe and S. Poppe, 'The Case for the Unity of Human Rights', *Bulletin of the GDR Committee for Human Rights,* no. 2/1986, p. 75.

11. Vladimir Kartashkin, 'The Socialist Countries and Human Rights', in K. Vasak and P. Alston (eds), *The International Dimensions of Human Rights,* Westport, Conn.: Greenwood Press, 1982, p. 636; see also Bloed and van Hoof, 'Some Aspects' (note 7 above), pp. 106–7; Chkikhvadze, 'Interstate Cooperation' (note 9 above), p. 92.

12. Farrokh Jhabvala, 'The Soviet Bloc's View of the Implementation of Human Rights Accords', *Human Rights Quarterly,* vol. 7, no. 4 (November 1985), p. 484.

13. UN General Assembly, *Official Records*, 183rd meeting, 10 December 1948, p. 925.
14. Bloed and Van Dijk, 'Some Aspects' (note 7 above), p. 66.
15. UN General Assembly, *Official Records*, 183rd plenary meeting, 10 December 1948, p. 927.
16. V. Chkikhvadze, 'A Socialist Conception of the Rights of Man: *Perestroika* and the Rights of Man in the USSR', paper for the World Congress of the International Political Science Association, Washington D.C., 1988, p. 23.
17. A.L. Adamishin, 'An Example of, and Hope for, International Co-operation: The Universal Declaration of Human Rights, Forty Years On', *Bulletin of Human Rights*, Special Issue, Fortieth Anniversary of the Universal Declaration of Human Rights, New York: United Nations, 1988, p. 7.
18. Mikhail Gorbachev, 'The Reality and Guarantees of a Secure World', *International Affairs (Moscow)*, 12 (1987); see also Peter R. Baehr and Leon Gordenker, *The United Nations in the 1990s*, London: Macmillan, 2nd edn 1994, pp. 149–50.
19. Amnesty International, *USSR: Human Rights in a Time of Change*, London, 1989.
20. For examples of anti-Amnesty publications, see Samuel Zivs, *Anatomy of a Lie* (1982); Oleg Vakulovsky, *The False Bottom of Amnesty International* (1987); Oleg Vakulovsky, *'Amnesty' With and Without its Greasepaint* (1988).
21. See *On Speaking Terms: An Unprecedented Human Rights Mission to the Soviet Union*, Vienna: International Helsinki Federation for Human Rights, 1988. See also Max van der Stoel, 'Human Rights in the Soviet Union', *SIM Newsletter Netherlands Quarterly of Human Rights*, vol. 6, no. 1 (1988), pp. 74–9.
22. International Herald Tribune, 12 December 1995.
23. See Edward N. Ozhiganov, 'The Politics of Russian Federation toward Ethnic and National Minorities', unpublished paper presented to PIOOM symposium

on 'Ethnic Conflicts and Human Rights Violations in Europe', Leiden University, 25 June 1993.

24. Address by A.V. Kozyrev to the World Conference on Human Rights, Vienna, 15 June, 1993.
25. Ibid.
26. Cf. Amnesty International, 'Russia: Armed Conflict in the Chechnyan Republic: Seeds of Human Rights Violations Sown in Peacetime', AI Index: EUR 46/10/95, April 1995.

Chapter 9 Western Europe

1. Andrew Clapham begins his book on human rights and the European Community with a quotation from Judge Pescatore: '[T]he builders of the European Communities thought too little about the legal foundations of their edifice and paid too little attention to the protection of the basic rights of the individual within the new European structure.' (Andrew Clapham, *Human Rights and the European Community: A Critical Overview*, Baden-Baden: Nomos Verlagsgesellschaft, 1991, p. 7).
2. Cited in *Human Rights Reference Handbook*, The Hague: Ministry of Foreign Affairs, 1992, p. 77.
3. Treaty on European Union, Title V, article J.1.
4. Cf. Johannes van der Klaauw, 'European Union', *Netherlands Quarterly of Human Rights*, vol. 12, no. 1 (1994), pp. 71-2.
5. See Francis G. Jacobs, 'European Community Law and the European Convention on Human Rights', in Deidre Curtin and Ton Heukels (eds), *Institutional Dynamics of European Integration: Essays in Honour of Henry G. Schermers*, vol. II, Dordrecht/Boston/London: Martinus Nijhoff, 1994, pp. 561-71.
6. Cited in *Human Rights Reference Handbook*, (note 2 above), p. 83.
7. Clapham, (note 1 above), p. 80.
8. Johannes van der Klaauw, 'European Union', *Netherlands Quarterly of Human Rights*, vol. 13, no. 4 (1995), pp. 458-61.

9.   Johannes van der Klaauw, 'European Union', *Netherlands Quarterly of Human Rights*, vol. 13, no. 3 (1995), pp. 279–81.

10. *Report on Human Rights in the World in 1993/1994 and the Union's Human Rights Policy*, European Parliament Committee on Foreign Affairs, Security and Defense Policy, 7 March 1995.

11. Cf. Johannes van der Klaauw, 'European Union', *Netherlands Quarterly of Human Rights*, vol. 13, no. 2 (1995), p. 179.

12. *Annual Report on Respect for Human Rights in the European Union*, 1993, Committee on Civil Liberties and Internal Affairs, 21 December 1994.

13. See Johannes van der Klaauw, 'European Union', *Netherlands Quarterly of Human Rights*, vol. 13, no. 2 (1995), pp. 178–80 and vol. 13, no. 3 (1995), p. 282.

14. European Parliament, *The European Parliament and Human Rights* Brussels: Directorate General for Research and the Human Rights Unit, 1994, p. 611.

15. Cf. Johannes van der Klaauw, 'European Community', *Netherlands Quarterly of Human Rights*, vol. 10, no. 2 (1992), pp. 206–7.

16. As derived from *Human Rights Reference Handbook* (note 2 above), p. 84; also World Conference on Human Rights, *Note Verbale dated 23 April 1993 from the Permanent Mission of Denmark to the United Nations Office at Geneva*, A/CONF.157/PC/87.

17. Cf. Johannes van der Klaauw, 'European Community', *Netherlands Quarterly of Human Rights*, vol. 11, no. 3 (1993), pp. 323–30.

18. Andrew Clapham rightly observes that these memoranda offer little if any information on concrete achievements. For a full record of EPC public activity he refers to the *EPC Bulletin*, edited by the European Policy Unit at the European University Institute (Florence) and the Institut für Europäische Politik (Bonn), which provides a detailed biannual record of all statements, declarations, questions, etc. related to the EPC. (Clapham, (note 1 above), p. 78, note 222.)

19. As quoted in *Human Rights Reference Handbook*, (note 2 above), p. 97.

20. Cf. Johannes van der Klaauw, 'European Union', *Netherlands Quarterly of Human Rights*, vol. 13, no. 2 (1995), p. 173.

21. Cf. William Wallace, 'Old States and New Circumstances: The International Predicament of Britain, France and Germany', in William Wallace and W.E. Patterson (eds), *Foreign Policy Making in Western Europe: A Comparative Approach*, Farnborough: Saxon House, 1978, pp. 31–55.

22. P. Byrd (ed.), *British Foreign Policy under Thatcher*, Oxford: P. Allan, 1988; Lawrence Freedman and Michael Clarke (eds), *Britain in the World*, Cambridge: Cambridge University Press, 1991; Michael Clarke, *British External Policy-Making in the 1990s*, London: Macmillan, 1992; Stuart Croft, *The End of Superpower: British Foreign Office Conceptions of a Changing World*, Aldershot: Dartmouth, 1994; M. Curtis, *The Ambiguities of Power: British Foreign Policy since 1945*, London: Zed Books, 1995; Daniel Verney, 'The Dilemma of French Foreign Policy', *International Affairs*, vol. 68, no. 4 (October 1992), pp. 655–64.

23. Philip H. Gordon, 'The Normalization of German Foreign Policy', *Orbis*, vol. 38, no. 2 (1994), pp. 225–43; Lothar Gutjahr, *German Foreign and Defence Policy after Unification*, London: Pinter, 1993; Günter Verheugen, 'Basic Issues of German Foreign Policy', *Internationale Politik und Gesellschaft*, vol. 3 (1995), pp. 259–67.

24. Helmut Kohl, 'Menschenrechte-Demokratie Entwicklung' ('Human Rights-Democracy-Development'), speech on 3 November 1986, *Bulletin Presse- und Informationsamt der Bundesregierung*, no. 134, p. 1121 (translated from the original German–PRB).

25. A. Burnett, *Iron Britannia: Why Parliament Waged its Falklands War*, London: Allison and Busby, 1982.

26. Transcript of address by the prime minister, Mrs Thatcher, to the College of Europe, Bruges, Belgium, on 20 September 1988.

27. Wolfgang Heinz, 'The Federal Republic of Germany: Human Rights and Development', paper prepared for the IPSA Hague Conference on Human Rights and Development, 1–3 June 1987, p. 5; *Menschenrechtsbericht der Bundesregierung, Reihe: Berichte und Dokumentationen*, Bonn: Auswärtiges Amt, May 1992, pp. 46–7.

28. Hans-Dietrich Genscher, 'The Foreign Policy of a United Germany', *The Fletcher Forum of World Affairs*, vol. 15, no. 2 (Summer 1991), p. 93.

29. *Menschenrechtsbericht der Bundesregierung*, (note 27 above), pp. 15–18.

30. *Menschenrechtsbericht der Bundesregierung für die 11. Legislaturperiode*, Bonn: Deutscher Bundestag, 1990, p. 14, as cited by Wolfgang S. Heinz, "Deutsche Entwicklungspolitik, Politische Konditionalität und Durchsetzung der Menschenrechte', in *EPD Dokumentation*, Frankfurt am Main, 14 May 1992, p. 19.

31. 'Die Menschenrechten als Grundlage Weltumspannender Zusamenarbeit', 'Human Rights as Foundation of Global Cooperation'), speech by Dr Klaus Kinkel to the World Conference on Human Rights, Vienna, 15 June 1993.

32. Cf. Heinz, (note 27 above), p. 35.

33. Amnesty International, 'Federal Republic of Germany: Failed by the System: Police III-Treatment of Foreigners', AI Index: EUR 23/06/95, May 1995; Amnesty International, *Report 1995*, London, 1995, pp. 138–9.

34. R. Barre, *Au tournant du siècle. Principes et objectifs de politique étrangère ('At the Turn of the Century, Principles and Aims of Foreign Policy')*, Paris: Plon, 1988, p. 178.

35. See 'La pratique française du droit international public', ('French Practice of International Public Law'), *Annuaire Français de Droit International*, vol. XXX (1984), pp. 982–989.

36. This secretariat has had numerous conflicts with the more conservative Ministry of Foreign Affairs. See Marie-Christine Delpal, *Politique Extérieure et Diplomatie Morale: Le Droit d'Ingérence Humanitaire en Question*

('Foreign Policy and Moral Diplomacy: The Right of Humanitarian Intervention Questioned'), Paris: Foundation pour les Études de Défense Nationale, 1993, p. 104.

37. 46th Session of the UN Commission on Human Rights, Point 11b, National Institutes for the Promotion and Protection of Human Rights, *Intervention de M. Paul Bouchet, Président de la Commission des Droits de l'Homme*, ('Intervention of Paul Bouchet, President of the Human Rights Commission'), Geneva, 1 March 1990.

38. *Annuaire*, (note 35 above), p. 984.

39. Speech by President Mitterrand at the celebration of the 40th Anniversary of the Universal Declaration of Human Rights in Paris, 10 December 1988.

40. Pierre Milza, 'Droits de l'Homme: le Combat de la France', ('Human Rights: The Fight of France') *Politique Internationale* 41 (1988), pp. 25–36.

41. Amnesty International, 'France: Shootings, Killings and Alleged Ill-Treatment by Law Enforcement Officers', AI Index: EUR 21/02/94; *Report 1993*, London, 1995, pp. 131–4.

42. *British Policy towards the United Nations*, Foreign Policy Documents no. 26, London: HMSO, 1978, pp. 14–26, as cited by R.J. Vincent, *Human Rights and International Relations*, Cambridge: Cambridge University Press, 1986, pp. 143–4.

43. Tim Eggar, 'The Universal Declaration of Human Rights – Forty Years On', *Bulletin of Human Rights*, Special issue, Fortieth Anniversary of the Universal Declaration of Human Rights, New York: United Nations, 1988, p. 31.

44. Speech given to the World Conference on Human Rights by Ambassador Martin Morland CMG, UK Permanent Representative to the UN at Geneva, 16 June 1993.

45. See Brian White, 'Britain and East–West Relations', in Michael Smith, Steve Smith and Brian White (eds), *British Foreign Policy: Tradition, Change and Transformation*, London: Unwin Hyman, 1988, p. 152.

46. See Amnesty International, 'United Kingdom: Summary of Human Rights Concerns', AI Index: EUR 45/06/95, August 1995; Amnesty International, *Report 1995*, London, 1995, pp. 289–302.

47. William Wallace, 'The Human Rights Factor in British Foreign Policy', unpublished paper for the second meeting of the study programme on human rights criteria in British foreign policy, 30 January 1979, p. 3.

48. While admitting that Community action *vis-à-vis* human rights in third countries is difficult to assess, Clapham nevertheless suggests that 'the Community may succeed where others fail'. (Clapham, (note 1 above), pp. 81–2.)

49. See Clapham, (note 1 above), p. 77.

50. Clapham has called the response by EPC to Parliamentary questions 'rather uncooperative' (Clapham, (note 1 above), p. 79.)

Chapter 10 The Third World

1. Jack Donnelly, *Universal Human Rights in Theory and Practice*, Ithaca and London: Cornell University Press, 1989, p. 50.

2. S.K. Agrawala, 'Human Rights: Some Problems of Developing Countries', in R. Guttierez Girardot (ed.), *New Directions in International Law*, Frankfurt, 1982, p. 377.

3. Yougindra Khusalani, 'Human Rights in Asia and Africa', *Human Rights Law Journal*, vol. 4, no. 4, 1983, p. 418.

4. S.A.A. Abu Salieh, 'La définition internationale de Droits de l'Homme et l'Islam' ('The International Definition of Human Rights and the Islam'), *Revue de Droit Internationale Générale*, 1982, p. 632.

5. Boutros Ghali, 'The Third World and Human Rights', *Bulletin of Human Rights*, Special Issue, Fortieth Anniversary of the Universal Declaration of Human Rights, New York: United Nations, 1988, p. 38.

6. Costa R. Mahalu, 'Human Rights and Development: An African Perspective', *Leiden Journal of International Law*, vol. 1, no. 1 (May 1988), p. 22.
7. Olusola Ojo, 'Understanding Human Rights in Africa', in Jan Berting *et al.* (eds), *Human Rights in a Pluralist World: Individuals and Collectivities*, Westport/London: Meckler, 1990, p. 117.
8. Rhoda Howard, 'Evaluating Human Rights in Africa: Some Problems of Implicit Comparisons', *Human Rights Quarterly*, vol. 6, no. 2 (May 1984), p. 170.
9. Cf. Evan Luard, *Human Rights and Foreign Policy*, Oxford: Pergamon Press, 1981, pp. 19–20.
10. Article 1, par. 2.
11. UNGA Resolution 41/128.
12. See Jack Donnelly, 'The "Right to Development": How not to Link Human Rights and Development', in Claude E. Welch Jr. and Ronald I. Meltzer (eds), *Human Rights and Development in Africa*, Albany: State University of New York Press, 1984, pp. 261–83. See also Subrata Roy Chowdhury, Erik M. Denters and Paul J.I.M. de Waart (eds), *The Right to Development in International Law*, Dordrecht/Boston/London: Martinus Nijhoff, 1992.
13. United Nations Development Programme, *Human Development Report 1994*, New York/Oxford: Oxford University Press, 1994, pp. 129–35.
14. Article 22.
15. Statement by Mr Ali Alatas, Minister of Foreign Affairs of Indonesia, to the World Conference on Human Rights, Vienna, 14 June 1993.
16. James Crawford (ed.), *The Right of Peoples*, Oxford: Clarendon Press, 1988, pp. 187–8.
17. Ian Brownlie, 'The Rights of Peoples in Modern International Law', in Crawford (note 16 above), p. 167; see also Marlies Galenkamp, *Individualism versus Collectivism: The Concept of Collective Rights*, Rotterdam: RFS, 1993, pp. 46–8.
18. Cf. Theo van Boven, 'The Relations between Peoples' Rights and Human Rights in the African Charter',

Human Rights Law Journal, vol. 7 (1986), pp. 183–94; Richard N. Kiwanuka, 'The Meaning of "People" in the African Charter on Human and Peoples' Rights', *The American Journal of International Law,* vol. 82 (1988), pp. 80–101.

19. Cf. Paul Sieghart, *The Lawful Rights of Mankind: An Introduction to the International Legal Code of Human Rights,* Oxford and New York: Oxford University Press, 1985, p. 164.

20. James Crawford, 'The Rights of Peoples: Some Conclusions', in Crawford, *The Rights of Peoples* (note 16 above), p. 167.

21. See Peter R. Baehr, 'Human Rights and Peoples' Rights', in Berting *et al., Human Rights* (note 7 above), pp. 100–1.

22. *Reservations, Declarations, Notifications and Objections Relating to the International Covenant on Civil and Political Rights and the Optional Protocols Thereto: Note by the Secretary-General,* CCPR/C/2/Rev. 3, 12 May 1992, p. 18; See also Sieghart, *The Lawful Rights* (note 19 above), p. 163.

23. *Covenant of the Unrepresented Nations and Peoples Organization,* Article 6.

24. Ibid, Article 5. The Representative Body of member-organizations '... shall mean a government, legislative body, liberation movement or other organ of leadership, whether in the territory of the Nation or People or in exile, recognized as such by a substantial section of the people which the Representative Body claims to represent' (UNPO Covenant, Article 6).

25. Maurice Cranston, 'Are There Any Human Rights?', *Daedalus,* vol. 112, no. 4 (Fall 1983), p. 9.

26. Hurst Hannum, 'The Limits of Sovereignty and Majority Rule: Minorities, Indigenous Peoples, and the Right to Autonomy', in Ellen Lutz, Hurst Hannum, Kathryn J. Burke (eds), *New Directions in Human Rights,* Philadelphia: University of Pennsylvania Press, 1989, pp. 15–16.

27. Cf. Julian Burger and Paul Hunt, 'Towards the International Protection of Indigenous Peoples' Rights', *Netherlands Quarterly of Human Rights*, vol. 12, no. 4 (1994), pp. 405–23.

28. See Richard Mulgan, 'Should Indigenous Peoples Have Special Rights?', *Orbis*, vol. 3, no. 3 (Summer 1989), p. 376.

29. See Advisory Committee on Human Rights and Foreign Policy (Netherlands), *Indigenous People*, Advisory Report no. 16, The Hague, 8 June 1993, p. 12.

30. United Nations, *Study of the Problem of Discrimination against Indigenous Populations*, E/CN.4/Sub.2/1986/7/ Add. 4, pp. 50–1.

31. United Nations, *The Rights of Indigenous Peoples*, Fact Sheet No. 9, Geneva: Centre for Human Rights, 1990, p. 3.

32. See Mulgan, 'Should Indigenous Peoples' (note 28 above), p. 387.

33. See Advisory Committee on Human Rights and Foreign Policy (note 29 above), pp. 7–8.

34. Bolaji Akinyemi, 'The Organization of African Unity and the Concept of Non-Interference in Internal Affairs of Member-States', *British Journal of International Law*, 1972/73, pp. 393–400.

35. Olusola Ojo and Amadu Sesay, 'The O.A.U. and Human Rights: Prospects for the 1980s and Beyond', *Human Rights Quarterly*, vol. 8, no. 1 (February 1986), p. 92.

36. Christian Much, 'Die afrikanische Charta der Menschenrechte und der Rechte der Völker' (The African Charter of Human and Peoples' Rights'), *Europa Archiv*, no. 1 (1988), p. 23. See also Richard Gittleman, 'The Banjul Charter on Human and Peoples' Rights: A Legal Analysis', in Welch and Meltzer, *Human Rights* (note 12 above), pp. 152–76.

37. Wolfgang Benedek, 'Enforcement of Human and Peoples' Rights in Africa: The Communication System and State Reporting under the African Charter', in

Jacqueline Smith and Leo Zwaak (eds), *International Protection of Human Rights, SIM Special,* no. 15 (1995), pp. 23–43.

38. Ojo and Sesay, *The O.A.U.* (note 35 above), pp. 97 ff. See also Ebua Lihau, 'Comments on the Banjul Charter', *HRI Reporter,* vol. 11, no. 4 (November 1986), pp. 12–15.

39. For instance, the length of time needed to respond to an emergency situation has been severely criticized by the International Commission of Jurists, as according to article 58 (3) of the African Charter a case of emergency must be submitted to the Chairman of the Assembly of Heads of State and Government who may request an in-depth study. See 'African Commission on Human and Peoples' Rights', *ICJ Review,* no. 47 (December 1991), p. 59.

40. Felice D. Gaer, 'First Fruits: Reporting by States under the African Charter on Human and Peoples' Rights', *Netherlands Quarterly of Human Rights,* vol. 10, no. 1 (1992), pp. 29–42.

41. Benedek, 'The African Charter' (note 37 above), p. 26.

42. Ojo and Sesay, *The O.A.U.* (note 35 above), p. 100.

43. See Josia M. Cobbah, 'African Values and the Human Rights Debate: An African Perspective', *Human Rights Quarterly,* vol. 9, no. 3 (August 1987), pp. 309–31; Much, 'Die afrikanische' (note 36 above), p. 23.

44. Cf. Lihau, 'Comments' (note 38 above), p. 15. See also Shadrack B.O. Gutto, 'Non-Governmental Organizations, People's Participation and the African Commission on Human and People's Rights: Emerging Challenges to Regional Protection of Human Rights', in Bård-Anders Andreassen and Theresa Swinhehart (eds), *Human Rights in Developing Countries, Yearbook 1991,* Oslo: Scandinavian University Press, 1992, pp. 33–54; Benedek, 'The African Charter' (note 37 above), pp. 34–7.

45. The proposed action programme consists of the following points:

1.	The OAU Assembly should publicly and regularly address violations of human rights in its member states;
2.	it should press member states to implement the African Charter;
3.	it should provide stronger support for the work of the African Commission;
4.	it should review the human rights situation when deciding whether to send election observers and whether an election is free and fair;
5.	it should ensure that human rights are an essential component of its work in mediating and conciliating conflicts;
6.	it should strengthen the African Charter. (Amnesty International, *Appeal by Secretary-General of Amnesty International to Organization of African Unity to Protect Human Rights in Africa*, June 1993, AI Index: IOR 63/04/93).

46.	Cf. Benedek, 'The African Charter' (note 37 above), pp. 37–8. For proposals to improve the procedure of the African Commission on Human Rights, see Anselm Chidi Odinkalu, 'Proposals for the Review of the Rules of Procedure of the African Commission on Human and Peoples' Rights', *Human Rights Quarterly*, vol. 15, no. 3 (August 1993), pp. 533–49.
47.	Hiroko Yamane, 'Asia and Human Rights', in K. Vasak, *The International Dimensions of Human Rights*, Paris: UNESCO, 1982, p. 651.
48.	See Khusalani, 'Human Rights' (note 3 above).
49.	Bangkok Declaration, paragraph 8.
50.	For some examples of the attitude of the Chinese Government at the conference, see Ineke Boerefijn, 'World Conference on Human Rights, 14–25 June 1993', *Netherlands Quarterly of Human Rights*, vol. 11, no. 3 (1993), pp. 293–301.
51.	See Yamane, 'Asia' (note 47 above), pp. 656 ff.
52.	Charter of the Organization of American States, article 3(j).

53. Marcelo G. Kohen, 'The Universal Declaration of Human Rights and Latin America', *ICJ Review*, no. 41, 1988, p. 44.
54. Cecilia Medina Quiroga, *The Battle of Human Rights: Gross, Systematic Violations and the Inter-American System*, Dordrecht: Martinus Nijhoff, 1988, pp. 93–111.
55. See David Forsythe, 'Human Rights, the United States and the Organization of American States', *Human Rights Quarterly*, vol. 13, no. 1 (February 1991), pp. 66–98.
56. E. Acevedo, 'Organization of American States: Additional Protocol to the American Convention on Human Rights in the Area of Economic, Social and Cultural Rights', *International Legal Materials*, vol. 28, no. 1 (1989), pp. 156–69.
57. Thomas Buergenthal, 'The Inter-American System for the Protection of Human Rights', in Theodor Meron (ed.), *Human Rights in International Law: Legal and Policy Issues*, Oxford: Clarendon Press, 1984, p. 442.
58. See further, Lynda E. Frost, 'The Evolution of the Inter-American Court of Human Rights: Reflections of Present and Former Judges', *Human Rights Quarterly*, vol. 14, no. 2 (May 1992), pp. 171–205.
59. In 1987 the Inter-American Convention to Prevent and Punish Torture entered into force. An Inter-American convention on forced disappearances was adopted in 1994.

Chapter 11 The Netherlands

1. Parts of this chapter have been published earlier, in David P. Forsythe (ed.), *Human Rights and Development: International Views*, London: Macmillan, 1989, pp. 154–70.
2. Cf. Philip P. Everts and Guido Walraven (eds), *The Politics of Persuasion: Implementation of Foreign Policy by the Netherlands*, Aldershot: Avebury, 1989.

3. Cf. Peter R. Baehr and Monique C. Castermans-Holleman (eds), *The Netherlands and the United Nations: Selected Issues*, The Hague: T.M.C. Asser Instituut, 1990, p. 1.

4. Joris J.C. Voorhoeve, *Peace, Profits and Principles: A Study of Dutch Foreign Policy*, The Hague: Martinus Nijhoff, 1979, p. 42.

5. Other so-called 'like-minded' countries are Canada, Denmark, Norway and Sweden.

6. Jan Egeland, 'Focus on: Human Rights – Ineffective Big States, Potent Small States', *Journal of Peace Research*, vol. 21, no. 3, 1984, p. 210.

7. Ministry of Foreign Affairs of the Kingdom of the Netherlands, *Human Rights and Foreign Policy*, Memorandum presented to the Lower House of the States General of the Kingdom of the Netherlands on 3 May 1979 by the Minister for Foreign Affairs and the Minister for Development Co-operation. (References are to be official English translation.)

8. See Jan Egeland, *Impotent Superpower – Potent Small State: Potentials and Limitations of Human Rights Objectives in the Foreign Policies of the United States and Norway*, Oslo: International Peace Research Institute, 1985, p. 9. He refers to *Om Norge og Internasjonale Menneskerettsvern*, Stortingsmelding no. 93 (1976–1977). The German Government published in 1992 a comprehensive booklet, *Menschenrechtsbericht der Bundesregierung* ('Human Rights Report by the Federal Government'), Reihe: Berichte und Dokumentationen, Bonn: Auswärtiges Amt, 1992.

9. Tweede Kamer der Staten-Generaal, vergaderjaar 1986–1987, 19 700 hoofdstuk V, nr. 125; Tweede Kamer der Staten-Generaal, vergaderjaar 1990– 1991, 21 800 hoofdstuk V, nr. 91. These papers are not available in English.

10. *Human Rights and Foreign Policy*, (note 7 above), p. 12.

11. *Human Rights and Foreign Policy* (note 7 above), pp. 138–9.

12. Tweede Kamer, vergaderjaar 1995–1996, 24 400, hoofd-stuk V, nr. 2, p. 49 (translated from the original Dutch).

13. Voorhoeve has mentioned a combination of four factors to explain the international-idealist tradition: inexperi-ence in world politics, pacifism, legalism and moralism. Of the last factor he writes: '[This] may be a combina-tion of the Dutch aversion to power politics, the reli-gious traditions in the country, a strong belief in the rule of law, and perhaps also a longing for influence and respectability which, because of the lack of power-political greatness, expressed itself in preaching to other nations how they should behave' (Voorhoeve, *Peace, Profits and Principles* (note 4 above), p. 50.) For a very critical view of the Dutch, at the time when a major segment of public opinion opposed the stationing of American cruise missiles on Dutch soil, see Walter Laqueur, 'Hollanditis: A New Stage in European Neutralism', *Commentary*, August 1981, pp. 19–26.

14. See C. Flinterman and Y.S. Klerk, 'The Advisory Committee on Human Rights and Foreign Policy in the Netherlands', *Netherlands Quarterly of Human Rights*, vol. 11, no. 3, (1993), pp. 283–92.

15. Royal Decree of 27 October 1981; law of 20 June 1984, article 2, paragraph 2.

16. Speech by Foreign Minister H. van den Broek at the inauguration of the provisional Advisory Committee on Human Rights and Foreign Policy, 21 April 1983, The Hague, p. 6.

17. Ibid, p. 7.

18. Almost all of these reports have been translated into English and can be obtained from the Secretary of the Committee at the Ministry of Foreign Affairs. The fol-lowing reports have been issued:
    1. 'On an Equal Footing: Foreign Affairs and Human Rights' (1984);
    2. 'Support for Human Rights: Suriname and Human Rights' (1984);
    3. 'Crossing Borders: The Right to Leave a Country and the Right to Return' (1986);

4. 'Freedom of Information' (1986);
5. 'Development Co-operation and Human Rights' (1987);
6. 'Threatened Women and Refugee Status' (1987);
7. 'Human Rights Conventions under UN Supervision' (1988);
8. 'Towards a Semi-Permanent European Commission of Human Rights' (1989);
9. 'The International Mechanism for Supervising Observance of the European Convention on Human Rights and Fundamental Freedoms' (1990);
10. 'Harmonisation of Asylum Law in Western Europe' (1990);
11. 'Democracy and Human Rights in Eastern Europe' (1990);
12. 'Human Rights and International Economic Relations' (1991);
13. 'The Human Dimension of CSCE' (1991);
14. 'The Traffic in Persons' (1992);
15. 'The Use of Force for Humanitarian Purposes' (1992);
16. 'Indigenous Peoples' (1993);
17. 'The 1993 World Conference on Human Rights' (1993);
18. 'Economic, Social and Cultural Human Rights' (1994);
19. 'Collective Rights' (1995).

19. Ph.P. Everts (ed.), *Controversies at Home: Domestic Factors in the Foreign Policy of the Netherlands*, Dordrecht: Martinus Nijhoff, 1985.
20. Ph.P. Everts and Guido Walraven (eds), *The Politics of Persuasion: Implementation of Foreign Policy by the Netherlands*, Aldershot: Avebury, 1989.
21. F. Grünfeld, 'Human Rights in Chile', in Everts and Walraven (note 20 above), pp. 269–81.
22. P.R. Baehr, 'The United Nations Convention against Torture', in Everts and Walraven (note 20 above), pp. 296–309.

23. F. Kremer and Alfred Pijpers, 'South Africa and European Sanctions Policy', in Everts and Walraven (note 20 above), pp. 310–19.

24. Tweede Kamer, vergaderjaar 1986–1987, 19 700, hoofdstuk V, nr. 125, p. 4.

25. M.C. Castermans-Holleman, *Het Nederlands Mensenrechtenbeleid in de Verenigde Naties* (Dutch Human Rights Policy at the United Nations'), The Hague: T.M.C. Asser Instituut, 1992. See also Peter R. Baehr and Monique C. Castermans-Holleman, 'The Promotion of Human Rights – The Netherlands at the UN', in Baehr and Castermans-Holleman, *The Netherlands* (note 3 above), pp. 23–34.

26. Marcel Zwamborn, 'Suriname', in Bård-Anders Andreassen and Theresa Swinehart (eds), *Human Rights in Developing Countries Yearbook 1991*, Oslo: Scandinavian University Press, 1992, p. 291. Caroline Ort, 'Suriname', in Peter Baehr, Hilde Hey, Jacqueline Smith and Theresa Swinehart (eds), *Human Rights in Developing Countries Yearbook 1995*, The Hague/Boston/London: Kluwer Law International, 1995, pp. 367–401.

27. See Amnesty International, *Report 1992*, London, 1992, pp. 141–4; Hans Goderbauer, 'Indonesia and East Timor', in: Bård-Anders Andreassen and Theresa Swinehart (eds), *Human Rights in Developing Countries, Yearbook 1993*, Oslo: Nordic Human Rights Publications, 1993, p. 137; Peter Baehr, Hilde Selbervik and Arne Tostensen, 'Responses to Human Rights Criticism: Kenya–Norway and Indonesia – the Netherlands', in Baehr *et al.* (eds), *Human Rights in Developing Countries Yearbook 1995* (note 26 above), pp. 57–87.

28. Press statement issued by the government of Indonesia, 25 March 1992.

29. 'Criteria voor het Reageren door Nederland op Schendingen van Mensenrechten in het Buitenland' ('Criteria for Reacting by the Netherlands to Violations of Human Rights Abroad'), *NJCM Bulletin*, vol. 11, no. 6 (September 1986), pp. 581–91.

Bibliography

This is a list of literature on human rights and foreign policy in English. The notes in the separate chapters contain more detailed references.

Alston, Philip (ed.), *The United Nations and Human Rights: A Critical Appraisal*, Oxford: Clarendon Press, 1992.

An-Na'im, Abdullahi Ahmed and Francis M. Deng (eds), *Human Rights in Africa: Cross-Cultural Perspectives*, Washington D.C.: The Brookings Institution, 1990.

Berting, Jan *et al.* (eds), *Human Rights in a Pluralist World: Individuals and Collectivities*, Westport and London: Meckler, 1990.

Bloed, A. and P. van Dijk (eds), *Essays on Human Rights in the Helsinki Process*, Dordrecht: Martinus Nijhoff, 1985.

Boven, Theo van, *People Matter: Views on International Human Rights Policy*, Amsterdam: Meulenhof, 1982.

Brown, P.G. and D. Maclean (eds), *Human Rights and U.S. Foreign Policy*, Lexington, Mass.: D.C. Heath & Co., 1979.

Cassese, Antonio, *Human Rights in a Changing World*, Cambridge: Polity Press, 1990.

Chodhury, Subrata Roy, Erik M.G. Denters and Paul J.I.M. de Waart (eds), *The Right to Development in International Law*, Dordrecht/Boston/London: Martinus Nijhoff, 1992.

Clapham, Andrew, *Human Rights and the European Community: A Critical Overview*, Baden-Baden: Nomos Verlagsgesellschaft, 1991.

Claude, Richard P. and Burns H. Weston (eds), *Human Rights in the World Community: Issues and Actions*, Philadelphia: University of Pennsylvania Press, 1989.

Crawford, James (ed.), *The Rights of Peoples*, Oxford: Clarendon Press, 1988.

Donnelly, Jack, *Universal Human Rights in Theory and Practice*, Ithaca and London: Cornell University Press, 1989.

Dundes Renteln, Alison, *International Human Rights: Universalism versus Relativism*, Newbury Park: Sage, 1990.

Eide, Asbjorn, Catharina Krause and Allan Rosas (eds), *Economic, Social and Cultural Rights: A Textbook*, Dordrecht/Boston/London: Martinus Nijhoff, 1995.

Forsythe, David P., *Human Rights and U.S. Foreign Policy: Congress Reconsidered*, Gainesville: University Press of Florida, 1988.

Hevener Kaufman, Natalie, *Human Rights Treaties and the Senate: A History of Opposition*, Chapel Hill and London: The University of North Carolina Press, 1990.

Hill, Delys (ed.), *Human Rights and Foreign Policy: Principles and Practice*, London: Macmillan, 1989.

Howard, Rhoda E., Human Rights and the Search for Community, Boulder, Col.: Westview Press, 1995.

Kommers, Donald P. and Gilburt D. Loescher, *Human Rights and American Foreign Policy*, Notre Dame and London: Notre Dame University Press, 1979.

Luard, Evan, *Human Rights and Foreign Policy*, Oxford: Pergamon Press, 1981.

Lutz, Ellen L., Hurst Hannum and Kathryn J. Burke (eds), *New Directions in Human Rights*, Philadelphia: University of Pennsylvania Press, 1989.

Matthews, Robert O. and Cranford Pratt, *Human Rights in Canadian Foreign Policy*, Kingston and Montreal: McGill-Queen's University Press, 1988.

Medina Quiroga, Cecilia, *The Battle of Human Rights: Gross, Systematic Violations and the Inter-American System*, Dordrecht: Martinus Nijhoff, 1988.

Meron, Theodor (ed.), *Human Rights in International Law: Legal and Policy Issues*, Oxford: Clarendon Press, 1984.

Muravchik, Joshua, *The Uncertain Crusade: Jimmy Carter and the Dilemmas of Human Rights Policy*, Lanham, Md.: Hamilton Press, 1986.

Newberg, Paula R. (ed.), *The Politics of Human Rights*, New York and London: New York University Press, 1981.

Pollis, Adamantia and Peter Schwab (eds), *Human Rights: Cultural and Ideological Perspectives*, New York: Praeger, 1980.

Ramcharan, B.G. (ed.), *Human Rights: Thirty Years after the Universal Declaration*, The Hague: Martinus Nijhoff, 1979.

Robertson, A.H. and J.G. Merrils, *Human Rights in the World*, Manchester and New York: Manchester University Press, 3rd rev. edn, 1992.

Rodley, Nigel (ed.), *To Loose the Bands of Wickedness: International Intervention in Defence of Human Rights*, London: Brassey's, 1992.

Ross Fowler, Michael, *Thinking about Human Rights: Contending Approaches to Human Rights in U.S. Foreign Policy*, Lanham: University Press of America, 1987.

Shute, Stephen and Susan Hurley (eds), *On Human Rights: The Oxford Amnesty Lectures 1993*, New York: Basic Books, 1993.

Tolley, Howard Jr., *The UN Commission on Human Rights*, Boulder and London: Westview Press, 1987.

Vasak, K. and P. Alston (eds), *The International Dimensions of Human Rights*, Westport, Conn.: Greenwood Press, 1982.

Vincent, R.J., *Human Rights and International Relations*, Cambridge: Cambridge University Press, 1986.

Welch, Claude E. and Ronald I. Meltzer (eds), *Human Rights and Development in Africa*, Albany: State University of New York Press, 1984.

Index